SMELL the
DIRT

SMELL the DIRT

and other
Life Lessons
Learned from
the Ground Up

LEON WEILAND

SANDY SPRINGS
PUBLISHING
Madison, Nebraska

For information, address the publisher:
Sandy Springs Publishing LLC
c/o Concierge Marketing
13518 L Street
Omaha, NE 68137

Paperback ISBN: 978-0-9860861-1-3
Kindle ISBN: 978-0-9860861-2-0
Epub ISBN: 978-0-9860861-3-7

LCCN: 2015901500
Library of Congress Cataloging Data on file with the publisher.

Cover photo:
Amber and Rob Photography
www.amberandrobphoto.com

Publishing coordination: Concierge Marketing Inc.
www.ConciergeMarketing.com

Printed in the United States of America.

10 9 8 7 6 5 4

To my beautiful wife and best friend, Jean, and my incredible kids. My life, faith, and dreams have purpose because of you.

CONTENTS

PREFACE

Rural Nebraska has been home to me virtually all my life. The pungent scent of freshly turned fields annually beckons me as it once did to a myriad of thick-bodied gulls migrating across the rural fields. They came by the thousands to follow the innumerable mow board plows being tugged along by post-war gas-guzzling, multi-colored farm tractors. Spewing cackling sounds from their exhaust pipes, they made their annual sojourn across the Eastern Nebraska farm fields creating a seemingly limitless amount of fresh ground to be picked over by orange and yellow beaks cawing and crowing, vying for the taste of another earthworm or field mouse. Their flittering here and there seemed to amount to no less than a celebration of new life and new hope.

I guess you can call me a farm boy, through and through. The smell of dirt turned by the spring plow will ever be implanted in my nostrils—as much a part of me as any part could be. I am who I am. No amount of money, wealth, or reputation I achieve can ever change that. It's certainly my belief that who we are in life is a product of our total life experience along with some genetic effect from those who gave us life in the first place.

So often I think people forget that.

INTRODUCTION

Many, many times my mother frustratingly exclaimed, "Lonny Joe, if your head wasn't attached to the rest of your body, I'm sure you would lose that too. Would you just keep your mind on what you're doing?"

You see, I'm a dreamer. To those who have little or no appreciation of this peculiar activity, it seems a waste of time. To those of us who dream, it's the life-blood of our existence.

As a high school student, my teachers commented on my high standardized test scores. They certainly thought I could have done much better than I did on my regular coursework. They did not keep it a secret that I didn't live up to their expectations. To me, there were always much more interesting things to study than the prescribed courses. The observation of life and its meaning has always been more interesting to me.

I have learned much, though not in the usual sense. I can read an entire book and remember few of the details yet at the same time be moved profoundly. I am not moved by life's small particulars. I am moved by the experience in its entirety.

In these pages I hope to give credence to the dreamers— the unconventional thinkers who many academics still determine will not turn out to be worth a damn. We are the remarkable few who see through the unimportant and have been astoundingly successful in many ways.

This book is intended to help the reader become stronger, more spiritual, courageous, lovable, compassionate, patient, and kind; to help you become richer in everything pure, clean, and powerful. Hopefully this book will help you develop the grit mindset required to lead the most purposeful life imaginable. God bless!

1

THE PARADOX THAT WAS MY FATHER

Six hundred people attended my father's wake service and subsequent funeral. We hardly had enough room for them all crowded in St. Leonard's Church. Gilbert Weiland had died September 29, 2001, from metastasized prostate cancer. I was fifty years old. I remember little about the weather that day except for the storm that brewed inside me. I just wanted get the whole ordeal into the past and move on with my life.

Farmers, friends, business leaders, shopkeepers. Down-to-earth, hard-working people, descendants of German/Irish immigrants from our typical rural community of Madison, Nebraska—they all came in their best coats and blue jeans to pay their respects to a man they held in high esteem for his virtues of honesty and integrity. In our northeastern Nebraska town, my father was considered a man of integrity.

Madison is situated along Highway 81, about two hours northwest of Omaha, Nebraska. When I was a small boy, there were three grocery stores in town, a shoe repair shop, three banks, two hardware stores, three beauty shops, a movie theater, and four beer joints. And about 1,600 residents, give or take.

Madison was typical of small town America, at least the small town America I grew up in. Its tallest landmarks were two grain elevators and St. Leonard's Church, visible to anyone who drove by on Highway 81. If you didn't have a car, the only way out of town was the bus. It stopped at the depot every day.

I stood in a receiving line across the front of church with my mother, three sisters, and two brothers.

For over an hour at the evening wake service different folks from the community expounded the virtues of this man. He had been generous with his time. He was loved by most everyone there.

Yet anyone who looked hard enough could see that Gilbert Weiland's adult children never said one word about him. We shed no tears for his passing. He had fostered little relationship with any of us.

I stood among hundreds of grieving citizens shaking hands and receiving their condolences but felt no grief. No one knew the chaos he had caused in our family. We did our part, as always, in covering it up.

I didn't miss him. I still don't. I'll always wonder how he could love us yet at times treat us so badly.

But let me start at the beginning.

As a boy I was constantly worried. I mostly worried about following the rules set down by the adults in my life. This relentless anxiety caused me untold difficulty as a child.

As a second grader I was invited to Mike Eulberg's birthday party. Mike was in the first grade, and my parents were his godparents. As I walked to his house that afternoon, I came to a crosswalk patrolled by Berny Kralik, one of the eighth-grade patrol boys. He was a real teaser.

He and the other seventh- and eighth-grade boys were in charge of sweeping the school hallways every afternoon after classes dismissed. Sometimes Berny let me ride around on his industrial-sized mop as he swept up and down the hallways. He said the extra weight made it clean better. Whether it did or not, riding on the mop was a good time, and I was proud to help.

When I came to the crosswalk that day and he stretched his arms out to block me from crossing the street, I just figured he was teasing me. I looked both directions and there was nobody coming, so I ducked under his arms and ran across the street toward Mike's house.

I was just about there when it occurred to me that maybe Berny hadn't been teasing. What if I was in real trouble? I was scared to death that he'd write my name down and give it to Sister Imelda, the school principal. The thought of such consequences put me in a state of panic, and I became physically sick to my stomach with worry as I sprinted back to Berny's intersection outside of school. By that time he was no longer on patrol duty, and I was forced to go into the school to find him. Luckily he was still there.

When I finally met up with him, I asked if he had written my name down. He looked at me in disbelief. "Heck no, I didn't write your name down. I was only teasing," he said.

Such is the mind of a nervous child. Sometimes the smallest problems cause the biggest worries.

I took all the rules seriously when I was a kid. I worried way too much for a child in grade school. I'd missed numerous days of school with stomach aches and nausea. There was a stretch of time where at recess I walked around the school yard alone for fear that if I played with the other boys, I might inadvertently forget the rules about not running in the school building and get reported. In retrospect, those were just episodes of extreme anxiety that affected me in a physical way. I never understood why other kids didn't sweat the same things I did.

On Friday afternoons, the patrol boys would come into our classroom and read aloud the names of any students whose names had been recorded during the week for misbehavior. These patrol boys were essentially glorified hall monitors, but for a second grader like me they may as well have been the Nebraska State Patrol.

Every student whose name was read aloud had to proceed down to Sister Imelda's office in single file.

I never found out what went on in her office because I never had my name written down, but I remember the sight of those patrol boys entering the classroom made me sick with worry.

Looking back I suspect much of my anxiety was caused by the expectations of my father to behave perfectly. Time and time again when report cards were handed out, my less-than-exemplary grades were overlooked. However, my grade in deportment was expected to be an A—and it was. I was terrified of what Dad would say and do if I wasn't well-behaved. It was a tough spot to be in as a little boy. The pressure was tremendous. I loved him then and I always will, but my dad could be one tough individual.

Who we are has so much to do with where we grew up and the family we grew up in. And that was never more true than with my dad.

He had grown up on a farm in the 1930s. He talked about families he knew without enough food to eat during those Depression days, let alone owning any luxuries to make their lives more comfortable. No doubt he was affected by the experiences he encountered as a child.

His goals in life were to own his own farm and build his own home. He had an incredible work ethic, a drive that was unrelenting and passionate. True to form, he accomplished those goals about the time I was a teenager. But for him that wasn't enough. He had to be in control of everything in his life—his work, his farm, and his family.

In addition to the farm, my father had a corn-shelling business. He owned a John Deere Model 6, mounted on a 1954 F6 Ford truck. This machine mounted on a truck chassis that removed the corn kernels from the cob. This voracious machine could separate over 100 tons of corn in a single day.

People in our community respected my father. He was a church-going man. He was never seen in a bar. He had a lot of friends and belonged to a card club. He loved to play poker. But most of all he was impeccably honest.

I learned the intrinsic value of such honesty when my father sold his farm machinery at auction upon retiring from active farming in 1990. On that sale he had a John Deere 4020 tractor. The John Deere 4020s were popular in the late 1960s and early 1970s. They had six-cylinder diesel engines and weighed over 8,000 pounds. In 1972, the last year they were manufactured, they retailed for around $10,000.

A gentleman came in before the sale to look at the tractor, and I watched my dad spend the better part of an hour telling the man everything that was wrong with his machine. To observe the conversation you'd have thought he was trying not to sell it. At the auction the man paid over $11,000 for it, which was a premium price for that tractor. I was bewildered.

After the sale, I approached the buyer to ask why in the world he'd ever pay such a high price for a tractor with all these defects. He told me that he knew these tractors inside and out and what problems to expect from them after a few years of normal wear and tear. My dad's tractor was no different. It was the fact that Dad had been upfront and honest that caused the man to feel comfortable with his purchase.

Here is the lesson: People will overlook your sins and defects; they will find a way to do business with you if you are respectful, honest, and forthright. Honesty, I believe, is one of the essential parts of a truly successful person. To be trusted is paramount. No one is successful by themselves. The cooperation of others is always required.

The honest guy who went to church and stayed out of the bars was the public Gilbert Weiland, the man the people of Madison loved and respected. But at home, my dad could be a real bully. Everything seemed fairly normal in my life until I was twelve.

I can still remember sitting inside watching cartoons one Saturday morning on our blonde Zenith black-and-white television set when my dad hollered inside and summoned my attention.

"Leon," he said. "Come out here and help me."

And so it began.

When I was a youngster, my dad went through several hired farmhands. Looking back, it's no wonder none of them stuck around for long. He verbally abused them. I recall his rants as he assaulted them if they made a mistake. The last one left when I was twelve years old.

So that Saturday morning I was called to come help. That was the day I turned into a man. Much of that turning into a man was becoming just as mean and abusive as my father, my grandfather, my great grandfather, and who knows how many Weiland fathers before that.

On that memorable morning Dad sent me outside, and with a scoop shovel and beet fork, I cleaned the manure from the hog shed. From then on I took the place of hired men who would not tolerate his treatment.

Cartoons on Saturday morning became a thing of the past.

2

WHEN ALL HELL BROKE LOOSE

My father's controlling manner was both abusive and intimidating. I felt as if every need or desire I had was of little or no importance. It seemed only the needs of Gilbert Weiland were important. Everyone in my family, including my mother, was forced to dance to his tune; there was simply no other way.

Even though she may have wanted to speak up, Mom was mostly quiet through all this. Several times she mentioned that if all the women she knew hung their wash (problems) on the line at the same time, she knew she would take her own back in. She obviously thought our family problems were more palatable than those of others.

The only time I felt loved was when I behaved absolutely perfectly and stayed on track. If I got off that track, even just slightly, *all hell broke loose.* I will use this term several times in this book. I believe it defines a situation in which there is clearly an assault that needs to be reckoned with to somehow waylay the consequential damage. My father would scream and holler and ask over and over why I was making his life so difficult, as if I was doing it deliberately.

Abusers control by intimidation and that was how my father operated. I incorrectly learned that the only way to have my needs met was through manipulation and control. If we wanted to talk to him about something, we'd have to do it through our mother because he wasn't able to communicate with his children on that level.

My father achieved a level of intimacy with people in the community that he did not achieve with his family. He didn't seem to have any problems conversing with others in town or being social with members of his card club, but he simply couldn't share that same openness with his own family—especially with his sons. Each one of us left home during one of his verbal outbursts.

I am hesitant to write about this, however, I feel I must to completely capture what it was like to live my childhood. As a very young boy I watched on numerous occasions as my father beat animals bloody with anything he could get his hands on in the event they refused to cooperate.

I can vividly remember one such time when a sow had built a nest in the southeast corner of the cattle feedlot to give birth to her piglets. Dad wanted to move her into the hog shed where they would be safe from the elements, but because she had already made her nest, she refused to go. The more he tried, the more stubborn she became. Even though her refusal to leave her nest was a natural and typical reaction, Dad beat that sow with a two-by-four–sized club until she relented. Her snout was bloody, beat up, and horribly swollen.

As terrible as it may seem, I learned to find this normal. As a result, I treated animals in the same fashion. I am sure many times I took my frustrations with my dad out on those blameless animals.

I do want to add here that my father never physically beat me. For this I am thankful. He must have drawn the line there somehow. There was definitely physical abuse among other branches of his family.

My father was both controlling and abusive. People with this personality trait tend to perceive virtually any words or action by members of their family, which is counter to their thinking or desires, as a personal attack. The typical response is a counter attack, be it verbal or physical, to get the offender back in line.

My dad did this and so did I as a young husband and father. There is little in my life of which I am more regretful and ashamed.

In defense of my dad's behavior, he grew up the son of Tony Weiland who had a temper. I only experienced this a couple times while he worked on our farm after he retired. It was an overwhelming, all encompassing and you-are-dead-if-you-don't-pay-attention sort of hot streak.

My grandfather rolled cigarettes using little two-inch by three-inch rolling papers dispensed in little orange packages purchased by my grandma along with Prince Albert tobacco dispensed from a hinged top, red obround metal can that fit snugly into the chest pocket of his striped overalls. Off the farm he smoked store-bought cigarettes with the filters on the end. He was a heavy smoker, which caused him to cough profusely, especially in the morning and when he was excited.

Nothing seemed to cause him more excitement than when he was in front of the TV watching "the fights," as he called them. He would sit within three feet of the TV screen, red faced, eyes bulging, fists clenched. Through that laborious cough he'd shout obscenities like, "Kill that son of a b----h." This man who headed the household in which my father was raised was not unlike many other Weilands.

I've been observing fathers for a long time now. It is amazing to me how many can seem so normal, yet when looking a little closer, you'll find an abundance of family dysfunction among their children. I have five siblings. Among us there have been seven divorces. I know of no household with a divorce rate as high where it was a wonderful place to live.

I am confronting generations of abuse and control in the Weiland family. This is where the buck stops. My dream is that my grandchildren will be the first generation of Weilands ever to grow up in an emotionally supportive environment where this crazy phenomenon does not exist. The buck stops here with me.

My mom, also forced to march to Dad's tune, was a gentle woman and I hardly ever remember her getting angry. I don't know if she ever grasped how my father's controlling manner affected me growing up. Yet she wasn't completely ignorant of my father's behavior. On numerous occasions she called him an "emotional cripple."

Here is another lesson: Abusers can always draw the line. I heard a story once about a medical doctor who would get drunk occasionally and beat his wife. One time after one of his tirades, she went to a photographer and had him photograph the bruises on her body. She gave one copy to a friend and one copy to her husband, with the promise that if he ever laid a hand on her again, or if she disappeared, a copy of these photos would be sent to every member of the medical profession in his city. Needless to say, he never hurt her again.

If you, the reader, are an abuser, emotionally, physically, sexually, or a combination of all, you can draw the line. You can stop as sure as the word is written on this page. Don't even entertain the thought that you can't. I am one, and I stopped. If anyone thinks here that I grew up in my father's house without becoming just like him, they are dead wrong. Abusive behavior is a learned behavior. No one is born with this knowledge. It is a matter of learning a new way, one that is not destructive to others.

If you are a victim of this abuse, you are also capable of drawing a line. They are called personal boundaries. No one has the right to cross them without your permission. If they do, put physical and emotional distance between you and them so they cannot hurt you anymore. If you are a parent, what are you teaching your children? I know what my parents taught me, and all I had to do was live there and watch them.

3

MADISON: MY HOMETOWN

As a youngster, I remember a lot of business activity in Madison, my hometown. We had two car dealerships, Ford and Chevy, both located in the heart of downtown Madison. There were always three to five filling stations where attendants would come out and pump your gas and check your oil—Conoco, Derby, and Phillips 66 and the Farmers Co-op Oil Company come to mind.

Alice Jones, an old maid, owned the bus depot in Madison. She sold pop, candy, and travel items such as shampoo, toothpaste, and combs. A newsstand there displayed the current edition of the *Madison Star-Mail*, the *Norfolk Daily News*, and the *Omaha World-Herald*, along with an assortment of magazines that included the girly kind that no one talked about. One of the local businessmen loved those magazines. He'd take free peeks until Miss Jones would ask him to either buy or leave.

Today the town is vastly different from what it once was. Most of those businesses have died out for the sake of progress. The beer joints remain, under new ownership of course. And the three banks are still there. But the three grocery stores have consolidated into one, as have the hardware stores. The building that once housed the Ford dealership was given by its owner to the local Knights of Columbus Council for use as a banquet and assembly hall. In short, the town has changed in the fifty-plus years since I was a kid there.

The farm on which we lived was a short three miles southwest of Madison, the place I have always called my hometown. The experience I gained as a child and later as an adult virtually all took place in this rural setting. My family, my church, and my school were all situated in and near Madison. I have lived and worked here nearly all my life.

We did not have a fancy home by any means, but we always had plenty to eat. Dad was adamant about that. He had lived through the Great Depression. He knew firsthand of families without enough food. He made sure that would never happen to us.

I wish I had understood more about that when I was young. Looking back, it seemed he may have worried much about that.

Even though he bought a new car for Mom to drive every four or five years, he didn't buy a second pickup truck for himself for nineteen years; he wore that old '54 model truck to the bone. By the time he retired it to the tree grove west of the chicken coop, it was beat up and rusted with big dents in its body and a cracked windshield.

I fabricated a story about the time Dad hauled a load of scrap metal to the recycler. While he was conversing with another farmer, the man on the crane nearly grappled up that old pickup truck because he mistakenly thought it was part of the scrap iron Dad brought in for recycling.

1954 International Pickup truck

I'm sure those youthful comments I made about that junky old truck were hurtful to him. They were funny to me. But I was unable to consider what he had done to acquire that old truck in the first place.

Because of Dad's corn-shelling business, he wasn't home much of the time. As a result, I was mostly self-taught. I just flat learned how to work, which is a priceless gift given to me by my dad.

It was no different for my younger brothers. In fact, it may have been more difficult for them because they had me to be the leader. They worked extremely hard on the farm when they were much younger than twelve.

My father worked us and worked us. However, we never worked any harder than he did. We learned the meaning of tough. I was not allowed to play sports when I was in high school because I was always at home working. My dad would never have allowed us time away from the farm for such frivolous activity. I do not think, however, that this was much out of the ordinary for farm boys at the time. I believe what was out of the ordinary was the manner in which he did it, along with his reaction whenever anything went awry.

Dad spoke numerous times about how his two younger brothers did a considerable amount of hell-raising in high school while he worked with his dad on the farm. Perhaps this is why he put little value on good school grades and such a high value on hard work.

I remember an occasion during my teenage years when I was visiting my friend Ron Schmidt. He, along with his brothers and his father, Harold, were having a conversation entirely about sports. They didn't talk about anything else, just sports. I just sat and listened; I can't say that I didn't have a clue what they were talking about, but it was certainly difficult to take part in a conversation with so little knowledge of the subject matter. I simply was never allowed the time to have an interest in anything that was not of interest to my dad.

My dad and I never talked about sports like Ron and Harold. We never really talked, period. That would have simply gotten in the way of getting work done.

I was intrigued by the father-son interaction. They carried on as if a conversation between a father and son was normal. I did not have that. It was simply not part of my life.

I think because of this, high school became the only fun part of my day. It became my reprieve from work. Because Dad did not put high value on good grades, I hardly put any effort into my schoolwork at all. I just floated by.

I always thought if I had put any effort into my studies, I could have been an A student. My sisters got extremely high grades. My youngest sister, Mary, was the class salutatorian. I've taken those Internet IQ tests, which prove I'm equally as intelligent. When I consider all I have accomplished, it must be so.

One teacher during my high school years always got my best effort. She taught English composition during my junior year. The first time I met Mrs. Hubbard I thought I knew everything. You know, seventeen years old, on top of the world, almost invincible, just sitting there in my desk in the northwest room of the second floor of the Madison High School "Old Building," talking to my buddies behind the top of an open desk.

Suddenly, there was silence. I looked up. There she was. The meanest, most vicious looking woman I had ever laid my eyes on. I remember exactly where I was. Two rows to her right and three desks back.

She was staring right at me. A cold shiver ran down my spine. She seemed six feet tall. She had sunburn everywhere except where she had been protected by a pair of wraparound sunglasses. All I could think about was how much she resembled a raccoon. But in my frozen condition, I could make no comment.

The first words I heard from her mouth were, "Shut your desks and shut your mouths, and pay attention!" It was as if God himself had spoken. Those words will forever be burned into my memory.

That day Mrs. Hubbard took control. She taught this rowdy high school boy to love writing. So effective was her teaching that, nearly fifty years later, I still remember many of her lessons.

She never asked for respect. She demanded it. She was exactly the kind of teacher I needed at that time in my life.

I believe that when we, as adults, gather together with our young people and do not help them to experience "love," then we somehow fail them. Mrs. Jan Hubbard never failed to help me in that experience. Her love and caring were the strong, tough kind, but they were love and caring just the same.

Mrs. Jan Hubbard

My life changed in response. With the skills I learned in her class, I was asked by the local newspaper to write articles covering the high school football games. Dad allowed me to do this as long as I had a ride to the away games. Because the coaches wanted the game reported in the local newspaper, I was allowed to ride on the team bus. This was the closest thing I ever experienced to being on a sports team.

Here is the lesson: Virtually everything is constructed from various components. Whether it be trains or airplanes or the computer you use in your office. No less can be said about anything that can be constructed from the written word. Just like bricks build buildings, words build compositions, essays, and books. But unlike buildings, which will someday fail, words gathered and recorded will last virtually forever. Be careful what you write. It is a permanent reflection of who you are. Words can be rescinded but never erased.

4

THE PLACE I COME FROM

Although people in my small community of Madison, Nebraska, may have respected what my father stood for in the public sphere, his farm was as cluttered as his dealings with his family.

While growing up, we lived in an old wooden house that hadn't seen its second paint job. My parents did not own that farm, but instead rented it from the Jacobson family, one of Dad's childhood neighbors.

When my father was a boy, his family lived on a farm adjacent and across the road to the north, while the Jacobsons lived on this one. I am sure that when my dad and mom moved there in 1951 the buildings were in a sorry state of repair—and they remained that way. My father probably saw little need to repair them. That would not have been part of any rental agreement. It would have been the responsibility of the landlord to make those repairs.

All the buildings on our farm had been built in the late 1800s. In the sixty-plus years of their existence, they had significantly lost their luster. Their paint was badly peeling or nonexistent and doors were falling from the hinges. Many of the windows in the out buildings were broken out allowing the industrious English Sparrows to build nests everywhere.

Our place was rather messy. It was embarrassing to live there, especially during my high school years. I never wanted any of my friends to come over.

The inside of our house was rather cluttered due to its small size and the size of our family. My mother liked crafts so there was typically an assortment of those items scattered around as well. That, combined with the fact that my dad seemed unconcerned with appearances, led to an array of discarded items cluttering our house and farmyard.

Prior to rural electrification in Nebraska during the 1940s, virtually all farms had some mechanical or gravitational means of supplying water to where it was needed. On our particular farm our well was equipped with a stroke pump, originally powered by a windmill, but converted to an electric motor by the time I was born in 1951.

Stroke pump

Next to the well was a 15-foot diameter by 3-foot deep, steel sided, open-top tank with a concrete bottom. The original bottom had rusted through years earlier. The sides were a series of moss-covered dents and tar-filled cracks, with an occasional leak around a hole that had been plugged with a small bolt, nut, and a couple rubber washers cut from a blown-out tire inner tube.

During the summer the water in the tank was layered with a crop of slimy green algae, floating here to there dependent solely on the direction of the wind—unless of course my siblings and I decided to take a cool dip on a hot afternoon.

Other than that, the surface was only disturbed by a column of water that trickled from the fill pipe, which coincided perfectly with the *cu-chooka, cu-chooka* sound of the stroke pump as it drew the cool clear water from beneath the ground, or an occasional ripple from the tail fin of a sunfish or bullhead that had unintentionally migrated there from the creek because I didn't take the time to prepare it for supper.

At the center bottom of this small reservoir was a drain line connected to watering stations in the cattle, sheep, and hog pens. It was attached at the center because this was the farthest distance from the circumference, which helped to prevent it from freezing solid during the winter months.

This supply tank required filling every couple days so it could continuously provide the animals with drinking water. The other factor that prevented it from freezing solid was the intermittent filling of the tank. The ground water pumped into it would thaw the ice except only on the very coldest of days.

This was not the case for the watering stations. They were much smaller and required supplemental heat. Kerosene lamps were kept burning beneath the small reservoirs where the livestock came to drink. Every Saturday afternoon during the winter months it was my responsibility to refill the lamps and clean the feed and poop residue left by the animals from the watering stations. This was a rather crappy (literally) job, to say the least. However, it was a job I could do. It was satisfying to know that the animals would have fresh drinking water because I was willing to do this menial task.

Here is the lesson: Serve with dirty hands, even filthy hands if necessary. Great intimacy with others is gained by coming into physical contact with whatever it is that makes them human. Performing these lowly tasks can give the doer one of the greatest gifts it is possible to receive, that of becoming "Holy as God is Holy."

Across the driveway from the livestock supply tank was where our house was located. Around it was a sagging, rundown woven wire fence intertwined with fire bush and pig-weeds. The rusty wire was precariously attached with intermittent bent-over staples to several leaning, semi-rotted cedar wood posts. The fence sagged from years of taking shortcuts over the fence instead of walking the extra thirty feet or so to the gate, which I would describe in much the same manner. It didn't sag from post to post, of course, it just sagged. It was constructed from two 1-inch by 1-inch rusty steel angles bent in a rectangular fashion to form the perimeter of the gate. The panel of the gate was no-longer-fancy braided wire mesh with triangular shaped openings. The latch did not work, of course, because the only evidence of a latch strike were the four holes and a rust stain on the post that once held the gate secure in the distant past.

The cedar wood post on which it hinged was rotted off at the bottom. A steel post retrieved from removing a pasture fence was driven into the ground immediately adjacent to it. The two posts were tied together with several strands of rusty baling wire wrapped around both posts a couple times at the top and bottom with the ends twisted together to keep it snug.

Baling wire was the fix-all on our farm—sort of like modern-day duct tape. Hay balers were commonly used to bind rectangular-shaped hay or straw bales. These bales are usually stored inside and used to feed or bed animals during the winter months. As the bales are used, most of the wire is typically bunched up and discarded or recycled. However because of its malleable properties it came in handy for fence mending, hose clamps, gate latches, and whenever anything needed to be secured. It was and is a must for any farmer repairman.

When I was a child, the only paint on our farm that I can remember was peeling off the buildings plus about twenty-five gallons of oil-based enamel in five tan-colored containers buried under a conglomeration of junk in the back of the tool shed. We threw the five-gallon bucket filled with hardened chunks of paint in with the junk preparing for my dad's farm sale shortly before he passed away in 2001.

In all my years as a child I never once saw my dad apply paint to anything. I wish I knew what it was about painting that escaped my dad's thinking. I always suspected it was left over from the Great Depression hardships of the 1930s. During that time in my dad's life there simply was no money for anything but food and basic necessities.

It seems he may have never completely recovered from the trauma of his youth. The thought of this surely gives me cause to ponder and to appreciate him much more. He was a real man. He did what he had to do to get the job done. Yet as a comfortably wealthy man, he lived as if he might not have enough money to last until the end of the next year. For that, I feel a sadness that he seemingly was unable to let go. Painting was a chore we simply did not do.

Just inside the front gate, about ten feet from the house was an underground root cellar. Every farm had one. Prior to rural electrification this was the only way to cool the food in the summer and preserve fruit and vegetables over the winter.

Our cave, as it was commonly called, was brick and plaster lined. Toward the front were two porticos, one on each side, about three feet by three feet and about three feet off the floor. These were used as shelves to store canned fruit. In the summer, potatoes, carrots, and other root vegetables were mixed with gravel and stored down there for use during the winter.

Unlike today, we did not buy anything at the grocery store that we could grow on the farm.

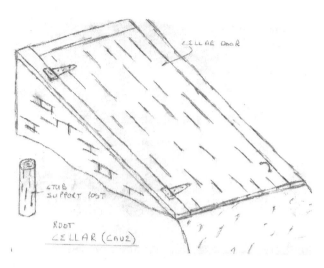

Sketch of root cellar

We did not have an apple tree on our farm so Mom purchased apples at DeGroot's Orchard. We would then wrap each individual apple in a piece of newspaper and store them in the cave with the vegetables.

In addition to being a storage unit, these cellars were also effective tornado shelters. We sought its refuge numerous times during threatening weather.

The cellar door was slanted about 30 degrees from the ground and when opened was supported by a stub wooden post protruding from the ground on the hinge side.

Since this door was typically closed, the top was rubbed slick from us kids using it as a slide. Mom picked numerous splinters from our rears when we'd veer off to the side where the wood was weathered but not polished.

The cave door was the only door on our farm I ever remember my dad replacing when it began falling apart. Leaving it in disrepair could have been dangerous had we fallen through it while playing. Also, it was the only thing protecting us from the wrath of a tornado.

Next to our house was a concrete-lined brick cistern extending eight to ten feet into the ground. The top of the cistern was concrete and hexagonal shaped, about six feet in diameter, and twelve inches high centered with a rusty steel manhole cover with the point of origin, Chicago, Illinois, cast in an arched fashion around the rim.

This platform supplied a baking surface for mud pies created by my sisters and me, provided they coaxed long enough. That was girl stuff, you see.

I never have been interested in the culinary arts, if that is what you call mud pies. Mud pies were made from dirt scraped off the barren dirt driveway loosened by passing farm machinery or scratching chickens wallowing in the dust on a hot afternoon. This fluffy soil was then sifted with a strainer fabricated from an old window screen that had fallen, dilapidated, from one of the sagging structures that populated our farmstead.

There is nothing quite like the feel of sifted dirt sliding between my fingers. I doubt there is any better ingredient than this if a smooth, lump-free mud pie is what you require on your imaginary taste buds.

During the late summer we, with our dirty faces, messy hair, and sweaty bodies sat around this concrete stump slurping watermelon while straining the seeds with our teeth and spitting them on the kid-worn ground that surrounded it and throwing the rinds as far as we could into the adjacent cow pen. The leftovers from these feasts were quickly devoured by ants and flies and washed clean by the next thunder shower, which didn't always happen too often during that time of year in Nebraska.

This reservoir contained the water supply to our house. The water was drawn up into the house by a green one-handed stroke pump mounted at one end of a four-legged sink. The sink had a curtain around the bottom that hid the cleaning supplies, some of which my mother bought from Mr. Meisinger, a door-to-door salesman.

To my siblings and me he was simply the Kool-Aid Man because in addition to cleaning supplies and brushes, Mom sometimes bought an orange drink concentrate mix in a half-gallon glass container. The backseat and trunk of Mr. Meisinger's car were packed with all his wares, which smelled like a mixture of kerosene and beauty soap.

Mr. Meisinger drove a black DeSoto with suicide doors. Engine noise and blue smoke smoldered from the underside where the exhaust pipe had rusted off. I remember my mother being excited when she heard the roar of his old car as it rounded the curve coming up the driveway we called the lane—a rather romantic name for a corn-cob–strewn road that connected our residence to the county road about a third of a mile across a dike and over a hill to the north.

These salesmen who traveled the farming areas were no doubt a connection to the outside for my mother and many other farm women who were semi-isolated due to living out in the country.

"Living in the country" may be a romantic notion for many today, but I doubt it meant much more than hard work and isolation for farm women during the first sixty or more years of the twentieth century.

Our sink was a red-rimmed, porcelain lined pan with a helter-skelter assortment of small, rusted patches around the outside bottom where the porcelain had chipped away from being banged against some hard object as the ice was knocked loose on a colder than normal morning. This pan was the universal water vessel for all to use. It was likely the precursor of the luxurious modern glass vessels seen in the latest additions of bath design publications.

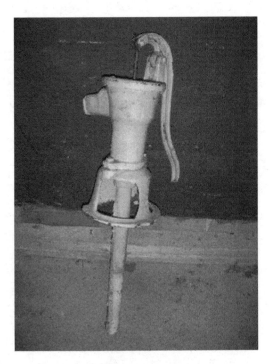

Vintage hand pump

The difference being that instead of simply turning the handle to acquire a steady stream of water at the perfect temperature, one had to pump the handle. The water temp was only perfect if you liked cold. If you needed something other, there was always an old calcium-encrusted pour kettle of hot water simmering on the adjacent cook stove to add a little heat to the water in the pan.

Mom always made us wash our faces and hands before a meal. There was a bar of lye soap in the corner of the sink that we used if we were being watched. We were always dirty, especially in the summer time. With no air conditioning, there was plenty of perspiration to make the dirt stick to our bodies. And stick it did!

The pump was coated with light mint green paint that was continuously flaking off and exposing the rusty iron beneath. Around the base was a layer of calcium and soap deposits left by evaporated well water and sloppy kids, splashed there from constant use. On the top was a dented and slightly out-of-round, aluminum cup commonly used by any and all who were thirsty.

The cistern was supplied water by a series of recycled water pipes, supported by discarded fifty-five-gallon petroleum drums and scarcely painted short pieces of wood from an old window frame separated from its former home by a strong wind.

This series of pipes began at the well by the big supply tank where water was delivered into the same cast iron cup connected to the fill pipe used to supply water to the supply tank; only to fill the cistern it was diverted 90 degrees. The first pipe with the cup was hung under the pump spout with a piece of corroded, galvanized wire. That inch and a half diameter pipe slid inside a two-inch pipe, which slid inside a three-inch one. These were shimmed with the wood pieces to create a sloped aqueduct in which the water ran from the pump to the cistern.

The pipes that crossed the outside yard across the driveway were stored in the weeds along the house yard fence. The pipes required to cross inside the house yard were laid in a more permanent fashion because they didn't require disassembling. My sisters, who seemed to never wear shoes during the summertime, used these as sort of a balancing beam, walking back and forth, gripping them with their bare feet.

The kitchen in our old house was painted watermelon pink—four walls and the ceiling, all watermelon pink! In the center was a table and chairs where we had all our meals.

On the north wall was a doorway accessing the hallway leading to the back door and the outhouse, and also where Mom talked Dad into dumping a pile of river sand, which he hauled from the sand pit by Norfolk in his pickup truck.

When the sand was first unloaded, the pile was three to four feet high and wet, which made the side of the pile steep and fun to play on. We played in this sand pile with our toy trucks and tractors. As the sand dried, however, it was much less inviting because there was little that could be made from it until the next time it rained. It would be like going to the beach and trying to form sand castles with dry sand.

About the only thing it was good for dry was tormenting my sisters by putting it in their hair. My sisters, however, added it as texture to the top of their mud pies. Not something I was inclined to do.

On Saturday night we all had to take a bath whether we needed one or not so we'd be presentable at church on Sunday morning. I remember being embarrassed once when I was about thirteen, when, for some reason or another, I divulged that at our house we only changed underwear once a week.

As I look back on those days as a youngster, I can't help but wonder if that was all that normal. I suppose there were other farm families who, as a product of a time without electricity or running water, had the same hygienic habits.

On the west side of that hallway was a four-legged, cast iron bathtub with only the drain plumbed. Since we did not have indoor plumbing until around 1960, in my early years we had none except for the pipe between the cistern and the kitchen sink. The bathtub drain went under the floor and led to a pipe protruding from the backside of the house where the water was dumped out onto the ground.

We only used this tub in the summer months because it was too cold in that room during the winter. Mom heated water to the boiling point on the kitchen stove and blended it with cold water to make a bath for us kids.

In the winter, we bathed in a red-rimmed, oval shaped, white porcelain lined pan about 24 inches by 15 inches near a heating stove in the house. Heated water was brought from the kitchen stove to put into this pan. When we were small children we stood in that pan while mom sponge bathed us.

When we got bigger, we sat on a stool with our feet in the pan and sponge bathed ourselves.

This must have been a fiasco with two adults and five children using this method to bathe. No wonder we only bathed on Saturday.

I don't recall having a bath in a full tub until after I was married. Even after the landlord installed indoor plumbing when I was about ten years old, I did not run more than a couple inches of water in the tub. At our house we were constantly reminded not to waste anything and that included water.

In the winter this same porch room is where Dad piled the carcasses of the dead animals he had caught in his traps while they waited for him to remove the pelts. He was able to store them there for a short time because they were usually frozen when he put them there and because in the winter, when Dad did his trapping, it was a very cold area of the house.

Also on the north side of our kitchen was a food pantry where various dry goods were stored. In this room we kept our cream separator. It was lime green, about four feet tall with a fifteen-inch-diameter tank with a cone bottom perched on three red wooden legs. On the side from top to bottom was a sight glass, which is a small window about three-fourths-inch wide running from the top of the cylindrical part to the bottom of the cone. At the bottom of the cone was a brass spigot with a butterfly-shaped thumb turn. The spigot was far enough off the floor in order to slide a five-gallon bucket underneath. On the top was a lid with a pull handle in the center, which prevented flies from getting into milk.

In order to separate the cream from the milk, Mom would take the fresh warm milk directly from milking the cows and pour it into the top of the cream separator. The heavier, more dense white-colored milk would settle to the bottom while the less dense, yellow-colored cream would rise to the top. After a couple hours a distinct line differentiating the milk from the cream could be seen in the site glass on the side.

This was a very low volume machine. It would maybe handle the milk from two cows. It was not electric but

Marvel gravity cream separator

worked on the principle that fresh cream and milk will naturally separate as described.

First, the milk would be drained off into a container placed beneath the unit by opening the spigot at the bottom draining the milk until the line separating it from the cream reached the bottom of the cone. The spigot would then be closed at the precise moment and reopened when a container to hold the cream was in place to collect the cream. The cream was used for making butter and baked goods while the milk we used for drinking. Because there was always more milk than we could drink, the rest was fed to the pigs.

On the east side of our kitchen, between the two long windows that looked out over the house yard, was our

Monarch wood electric combo stove

cook stove. This is where my mother did all her cooking. The righthand side had four electric burners and an electric oven much like many of the modern kitchen ranges used in homes today. The lefthand side however, was different. This side had a cast iron top over a fire-box where we burned corn cobs to heat the cooking surface.

On the west kitchen wall, a door led into the living/dining room. The terms *living room* and *dining room* were interchangeable at our house. This room was used for dining only when we had company for events such as baptisms and birthdays. The rest of the time it is where all the family activity went on if we weren't in the kitchen.

The painted wood trim around the doorway between the kitchen and the dining room was chipped and dented because Mom allowed us to ride a tricycle back and forth with a steel axel protruding from the center of the back wheels. Mom was as easy on us as Dad was hard.

In the winter a fuel oil stove beside the door to Mom and Dad's bedroom on the north side of this room provided the only source of heat for our entire house except for the corn-cob burner in the kitchen. This is where we sponge bathed during the winter.

Directly above this stove was a ceiling register, which, when it was open, but never was, allowed heat into my sisters' room directly above. Numerous times Dad yelled upstairs to my sisters to, "Shut the register! Do you expect us to heat the whole house?" Heat was another thing we didn't waste.

While my sisters' room was always above the dining room, mine was across the hall on the north side of the house above the back hallway. This was the hottest room in the summer and the coldest in the winter.

During the summer months Mom gave me a fan to use to keep somewhat cool as I went to sleep. However, I was to turn it off just before falling asleep and thereby save electricity. Being the boy who followed the rules, I did so religiously. At our house we didn't waste electricity either. Because this room faced the cold north wind, during the winter Mom always put flannel sheets and a wool quilt on my bed.

The window next to my bed was rather rickety and leaked around the edges. After a snowstorm, I typically had a little snowdrift up to an inch high across my bed. Usually I just brushed it off onto the floor where it seemed to disappear. One time though, I left it there to see how long it would last if I never disturbed it. It stayed there for over three weeks before, on a warmer than normal day, it melted and evaporated. My room was cold!

My brother's room was facing the east toward the cattle pen where there was an eight-foot in diameter water tank used by the cattle who roamed in the pasture and the grove of trees that bordered the north side of our farm place. During the summer months the cattle lounged in the trees and came to drink from this tank.

Beyond this pen was Mom's garden where she grew vegetables for our family dinner table.

The walls in my two younger brothers' room, along with all the rooms in the upstairs of our house, were slanted up and in from about four feet from the floor. On the north wall of this room a door led to an attic area. Mom stored "stuff" in there.

Bottle and arbor press

I recall bottles and bottle caps, along with an arbor press used to press the caps on the bottles. We once used this equipment to make root beer. I do not recall how that went as I was typically not interested in the preparation of food or drink of any kind. However I was fascinated by the tool used to install those caps.

Also in that attic area was an old 16-gauge single shot shotgun with a bent barrel. It once belonged to my grandfather, Tony Weiland. The stock had been taped together with black friction tape but the hammer would not stay cocked. It looked as if it had been run over by a truck and stored in a corn crib. In addition there was a wooden box that contained a shoe repair kit, including a shoe repair anvil. This fascinating tool caught my attention.

As a small boy this same room was used by my father as a makeshift shop where the pelts from his trapping business were processed and stored. After that it was the room where the hired man slept. It was only later that the room was used as a bedroom for my brothers.

When I was very young, the dining room floor was covered with flowery linoleum. Later it was changed to a more subdued neutral pattern. On the south side of the room was a bay window with white sheer curtains. Above them was a big patch where the roof had leaked, ruining the plaster. In addition to a pink sparkly couch and gray overstuffed rocking chair, Mom had a blonde dining room set and desk they had purchased in Omaha.

Dad invariably shipped his fattened cattle to the Omaha Stockyards, which was about a hundred miles away, where they were bought by one of the various meatpackers in the area. The cattle would be picked up by a cattle truck and transported to Omaha to be sold. On the day before they were to be sold, Dad would typically exchange the mud tires on the car with street tires. The mud tires made a howling sound because of their aggressive tread design. The next day he would drive to Omaha because Dad wanted to be sure the commission company, with whom he contracted to sell them, worked hard at getting him the best price.

One particular time he sold cattle, Mom and I went along. While Mom waited in the commission company's office, Dad let me go out into the cattle yards with him. Unlike the farm, where to be among the animals one had to walk in the mud and manure, at the stockyards all the walkways were on top of the fences. Walking around on the fence top runways was a delight for me.

Beebe and Runyan furniture store

On this particular trip, after the cattle were sold and Dad received his money, we all went in the car to downtown Omaha to the Beebee and Runyan Furniture Store. There, my parents purchased the blonde-colored dining room set, which included a table, six chairs, and a china hutch. In addition, they also purchased a writing desk. Mother was ecstatic. I think this was the first new furniture she ever had.

Several weeks later I went with Dad to the train depot in Madison where we unloaded the wooden crates off a box car and into the pickup truck. I doubt I was much help because I was only five or six years old at the time. I remember the excitement as the crates were opened and the new furniture was set in the dining room.

Behind our house was a rustic, two-hole outhouse. Inside, the four walls were no more than the two-by-four studs that held the exterior unpainted siding in place and a roll of tissue attached to a wall stud on the east with a rusty piece of number nine wire and a sixteen-penny nail.

This small wooden building with nothing but a semi-rotted wooden foundation straddled a hole dug in the ground. The toilet seats amounted to a couple holes sawed into a double two-by-twelve, which stretched from one side to the other. The sharp edges around the two holes had originally been hewn down with a half round wood rasp and subsequently been polished by the back sides of numerous visitors. In addition to the various insects that surrounded it, there was always an old Sears and Roebuck catalog on the seat, with some of its pages ripped out for use as emergency toilet paper in the event the store-bought roll ran out.

The cracks in the siding along with the dilapidated door allowed light to stream in during daytime use. At night we used a flashlight, but only to light the way there and back. At night business was done in the dark to save the flashlight batteries for more important uses. I have never been able to totally rid myself of the apprehension of leaving a flashlight on when there is no need to see in the dark.

To access this little mansion from the back door of our house, one was required to navigate a series of recycled wooden boards that sat precariously on the path. During the summer the cattle grazed this area. So if it had rained, it was necessary to stay on the boards and thus stay out of the mud—and to dodge any piles of cow poop that had been deposited on the boards.

During the winter when the ground was frozen, it didn't matter. If there was snow on the ground, we simply tromped a path through the snow. I don't ever recall anyone scooping the snow from the path.

This was a rather crude outhouse model. Our neighbors, Mike and Dot Wessel, on the other hand, had a concrete walkway going to their outdoor toilet. Not only that, but an electric light hung above, which made it possible to read even at night. Their door was straight and let in no light. The inside was lined with sky blue painted wainscoting. And it was equipped with an electric heater. I was impressed. As a boy I hoped to have a toilet house like that someday. It was definitely a cut above ours.

Behind the outhouse a dense grove harbored an old stripped-down truck body. The engine, front fenders, and doors were missing, along with the seats, glass, and truck bed. It was covered with rust and white splotches of bird poop and faded patches of black paint that refused to surrender to the wind and rain. All around, the corners were polished to the bare metal by the cows rubbing themselves from an itch.

It was in this junked-out truck body that my sisters and I stacked some old wooden apple crates for use as seats and took imaginary trips to California, Sioux City, and other far-off places. I would ask, "Where are we going?" Linda would reply, "California."

We'd make engine sounds by trilling our tongue and cranking the old steering wheel back and forth while the sun sparkled through the dense elm trees above and the breeze blew through the open holes where the doors and windows once were. What great fun that was. We were only hindered by what we could not imagine.

Here is the lesson: Teach imagination. All the knowledge in the world does not compare to the products of people with great imaginations. A man once told me that it is easy to make something when all the right materials are available. It gets much more difficult to do when all you may have is a hodge-podge of various pieces of discarded junk.

On the south side of our house adjacent to the kitchen was an enclosed porch with a series of coat hooks where we hung our everyday clothes. The only closet in this house was in Mom and Dad's bedroom. I guess the people who built this house did not have many clothes. Considering that some of the houses of this vintage were built by people who previously lived in a dugout or a sod house, a house with only one closet most likely would have seemed like a mansion.

The porch floor was typically littered with an assortment of stuff, for lack of a better word. The walls were painted white like the rest of the exterior of the house except they hadn't experienced fifty or so years of exposure to the weather. The floor boards were in the same condition except where they protruded to the outside of the exterior door. On the inside of the door they were still painted. On the outside they were weathered and worn.

In the summer my mother used this area as a wash room. Every Monday she would roll the old Maytag ringer-type washing machine and two rinse tubs to the center of the porch. The washer was filled with heated water from the kitchen stove along with a cloth sack filled with chunks of

Maytag ringer-type washing machine

homemade lye soap. The rinse tubs were filled with cold water pumped directly from the cistern via the hand stroke pump.

She would gather all the dirty laundry together and begin her Monday washday routine. White wash first, colored clothes second, and the dirtiest work clothes last.

After washing she simply, one by one, pushed the washer and rinse tubs to the door, dropped the drain hoses from their hooked positions and let the water run on the ground in front of the house. Where the discarded lye soapy water ran on the ground in front of the house was about the only place we didn't have weeds. In fact nothing grew there in the dirt except a few misplaced gravel stones.

I was always intrigued with the ringer part of that machine. It had two rubber rolls, one black and one white, which were powered by an electric motor. They were used by the operator to squeeze the water from the wet clothes that were fed between the rolls as they rotated tightly together in opposite directions, pinching the laundry between them as they rotated. They would also pinch fingers as well if the operator was not careful.

I always wondered why Monday was laundry day. I suspect it had something to do with the fact that we wore the same clothes, underwear included, all week.

5

LEARN FROM OTHERS

Uncle Arny and Aunt Therese, my mother's only sister, lived on a farm several miles northeast, near Enola. The farm buildings were dilapidated and paint was nonexistent. Ducks and geese were running everywhere, and the floors in their house were strewn with a thin layer of gritty sand tracked in from the barren ground around their house by their seven children.

There was no concrete sidewalk leading to their house, but instead a rotted boardwalk led to their front door. The board walkway connected the house to the well, which was about thirty feet from their door. They had no running water of any sort. If you needed water, you carried it from the well in a porcelain-lined bucket. A metal cup was used to dip water from the bucket when anyone needed a drink. A dirt path strewn with animal poop led to the outhouse about fifty feet east of the front door on the edge of a mulberry grove.

Their farm was populated with fifty or so acres of trees, many of them mulberry. There were mulberries everywhere. When we would visit, the bottoms of our bare feet would be stained purple from stepping on the berries that had fallen from the trees. In addition the berries were great fodder for the numerous birds that made their homes there, along with the ducks and geese. Those animals sure left a purple mess, if you know what I mean.

But for me, Uncle Arny and Aunt Therese's farm was the freest place in the world, especially compared to the world I was accustomed to.

A couple of times I was allowed to stay a day or two with my cousin David. While I was there, absolutely nothing seemed to curb our imagination.

David was the second youngest in their family of seven kids. He was the only boy. We'd have nothing but fun. We'd start the days watching cartoons after which we'd rummage about in their old farm buildings and climb trees and explore in the woods the rest of the day. We also spent a considerable amount of time tormenting my girl cousins.

I learned from my mother that Uncle Arny had attended college for two years after he graduated from high school. I guess you could say he was an educated guy, at least by our family standards. Whether or not he chose to be a farmer, I don't know.

I think in rural Nebraska during the 1930s many people did not have the privilege of choosing their profession. Instead they did what was necessary to feed their families. I like to think that is how my uncle became a farmer, even though maybe this was not his calling.

Uncle Arny was ingenious. Back in the days when TV antennas required rotating to get better reception, he salvaged a rusty iron steering wheel from an old truck and mounted it on his living room wall. It was attached to a shaft that protruded through the wall and was attached to two bevel gears, which in turn were attached to the pole that held the TV antenna. If the feed on the TV was fuzzy, the viewer could rotate the steering wheel right or left until the signal improved. How cool was that?

He made all sorts of gadgets like this. He fabricated a playground swing from recycled well pipe. My cousins had the tallest playground swing I had ever seen. The heavy steel end supports were bored several feet into the ground, and the top cross section was welded into place like a steel girder at a construction site. This was a rock solid piece of equipment.

Because of its height I discovered that at the top of the back swing, if I would snap the chains supporting me, I would be propelled, seat and all, into a free fall to be caught just before it came to the bottom of the swing arch. This stunt was just like flying—at least to a little boy.

I was always fascinated with the things Uncle Arny devised. He was an inventor; that much is certain. He could make "it" from whatever was at hand, even if that "at hand" was only discarded scrap iron.

Uncle Arny had a positive effect on my childhood. I made my first workable wheelbarrow from an old nail keg and a discarded tricycle wheel he gave me. He was gentle and kind. I always admired him. He was the first man I encountered who loved what I later came to love as well, building and BS.

He told a story about shooting a crow with a 12-gauge shotgun from a distance so far away he could barely see the crow. And when he went to make sure the crow was dead, the only things he found were the left wings. It was a fun story. Uncle Arny knew it was BS and everyone else, including little me, knew it as well.

On the other hand, compared to our home and Uncle Arny's cluttered farmyards, our neighbor's farmstead was just the opposite. Bill and Mabel Mazuch's farm was next door to ours. While they may not have been as well off financially as my father, I thought they were rich.

Their home was always immaculate. Their house and the other buildings on their farm always had a fresh coat of paint, and their lawn was precisely manicured. There were flowers and trees planted in neat patterns, and the inside of their house was a lesson in interior design.

Mabel loved to refinish old furniture. All the right pieces were tastefully distributed about their home.

Mabel was the only person I knew, other than Uncle Arny, our priest, and school teachers, who was college educated. She could speak French and she was from the city, Beaumont, Texas, I believe, which certainly was an anomaly in rural Nebraska.

Bill and Mabel met while Bill served in the military. They seemed to be an unlikely pair.

I decided that when I grew up and had a place of my own, I'd want it to be as nice as Bill and Mabel's place.

I noticed the differences in other families too. Riding in family cars other than our own was another lesson in tidiness. Nobody else seemed to have the quarter to half inch of dried mud on the floorboards, and the outsides of their cars were clean. In all my years at home I never once saw my father wash one of our vehicles. I took a girl to the prom in a filthy car because I was afraid to ask permission to wash it. I was embarrassed, to say the least, but that was how it was.

Here is the lesson: Learn from others. They all have something to teach. You can learn just as well from what they do well as from their failures. I have learned that just as many family troubles are caused by an obsession for perfection as the absence of caring at all.

6

THE POWER OF IMAGINATION

During my teen years when the other kids were learning how to play ball, I learned how to drive our tractors and our old, faded green, dented 1954 International pickup truck. I learned how to back two- and four-wheeled machinery with the tractor. I learned how to hand-milk the cow, grind corn for livestock feed, tune up engines, service the equipment, weld steel, build and fix fence, and repair about anything that was broken.

During the summer I learned how to cut thistles and cockleburs and harvest the alfalfa hay. If there was a job to do on our farm, I could do it.

My dad always made sure the power trains on our farm equipment were serviced religiously because their failure would add up to a costly repair bill. However, everything else was mostly left to the whims of the elements. The seats were cracked and in disrepair, and if there was a way to stop a tractor without using the brakes, that is how it was done.

We had an F10 Farmhand loader mounted onto the front end of a Model 44 Massey Harris tractor. We used this machine to stack bunches of hay that had been swept together by another machine called a hay sweep. It was

Model 44 Massey Harris tractor and loader

hydraulically powered and allowed us to create tall stacks of hay by piling the small bunches.

By the time I was fourteen, I was conscripted to operate this machine—a dangerous job because the tractor on which it was mounted had faulty brakes. Farm tractors typically have two brakes, one for each of the back wheels. Used together, they operate the same as in an automobile. Used separately, in addition to the steering wheel, they aid in turning the tractor one way or the other. As it was, one brake did not work at all and the other was weak.

This tractor also did not have what is commonly called live power, meaning that power to both hydraulics on the loader and the power to the wheels were not separated.

This allowed the weight of the hay bunch on the loader to be used in slowing and stopping the tractor, which was a rather handy method of controlling the speed of a tractor with brakes such as this.

Looking back on it now, it seems rather incredible that I was allowed to operate a defective piece of machinery. However, I can only surmise that my dad was a product of his upbringing. During his childhood in the 1930s there simply was no money for anything unnecessary. He was used to going without; it was acceptable to him.

In addition, I do not believe it was outside of the common thought at that time to have operational machinery with such hazardous defects. Consider that automobiles in the 1950s had literally no safety features. At that time I believe folks were still reveling in the luxury of having a machine, whether automobile or farm tractor, which didn't require hay to eat. After all, cleaning up horse poop or being kicked in the face by an animal wasn't all that safe or inviting either.

On a positive note here, I think learning to use whatever was available to get the work done was a priceless gift to me from my dad. He forced me to use my imagination so I could accomplish what needed to get done. I have used that imagination time and time again throughout my life. It has enabled me to attain goals I never thought imaginable.

Did my father intend to give me that gift? What difference does it make? It was there, so I took it.

Here is the lesson: It seems that maybe too much is made about intentions when it comes to fathers and sons. Sons can glean valuable lessons from their dads, no matter what the father's intentions are. It is important to be watchful and mature in thinking. Every man, no matter his disposition, has valuable life experiences. A wise individual can glean some valuable lessons just by watching others. Mine them like gold and move on. Don't get stuck in the semantics. That will do nothing other than hold you back.

If you have tasted the luscious flavor of roasting ears of sweet corn, grilled on the Fourth of July, you most likely left the cob on your plate to be thrown out with the garbage. Even though this delicious food is only a relative to the massive acres of corn that have been grown on Midwestern farms for a century or more, the two main components of the corn ear are the same.

The modern corn harvesting machine is commonly called a combine because it combines several tasks previously done one at a time. These contemporary machines are typically GPS guided and capable of harvesting hundreds of tons of corn per day. The central computer on these machines monitors the numerous operations comprising their many working parts—making them an example of the efficiency that has been achieved in modern American agriculture.

However, prior to the combine, the ears of corn, so called because they protrude out from the main stalk like ears, were stripped from the stalk with a machine called a

Corn picker

corn picker. This machine was mounted on a farm tractor driven down the ripened corn rows.

On each side of "the picker" was a pair of "snapping rollers," which rotated in opposite directions and perpendicular to the corn stalk. As the machine moved forward down the corn row, the corn stalks were directed between these rollers. Because the space between the roller was only wide enough to accommodate the diameter of the stalk and not the corn ears, the ears were snapped off and delivered to a conveyor that ran parallel to the snapping rollers. The ears were then transferred to a barge wagon towed behind. When the wagon was full, it was unhooked from the picker and attached to a farm tractor and pulled to the corn crib.

Corn elevator

The corn was dumped into a machine commonly called an elevator that conveyed the ear corn into a corn crib for further drying. The sides of the crib were perforated to allow air to pass through the stored ear corn.

Corn sheller

After further drying, the ear corn was unloaded from the bottom of the crib and into a conveyor that transferred it into a machine called a corn sheller, which my dad owned.

There were three byproducts of this process: shelled corn that was transferred from the corn sheller into a truck or barge wagon and delivered to another building on our farm called a granary for later use as livestock feed; corn husks, commonly called shucks, which were typically burned but sometimes used for livestock bedding; and cobs, which were unloaded from the sheller into a barge wagon and then unloaded into bumpy mounds along our one-third-mile-long driveway to prevent car and truck traffic from getting stuck in the brown Nebraska mud. Cobs were also fuel for the kitchen stove.

About fifty feet south across the driveway in front of our house was "the cob shed"—connected to our house by a concrete walkway half buried by dirt discarded from mud-encrusted farm implement tires passing between the two buildings.

The south half of this building was filled with a conglomeration of all sorts of things. The bare two-by-four stud walls were adorned with several old, dusty cloth sacks of brome grass seed, several bundles of steel animal traps, and obsolete parts of various machines, which once proved useful around our farm, all of which were mixed with cobwebs and residue that had fallen from sparrow nests as the doors were broken and never tightly closed.

In the southeast corner sat an old International Milk Separator on which hung a bent chicken feeder that someone intended to repair but never did. In the back was a

Green stamps

pile of fifty-pound sacks of Cooper Chicken Feed, with the promise of items that could be ordered from the S&H Green Stamp Catalog, simply by tearing the coupon from the sack. As long as Mom had chickens, she bought Cooper Feed—I suspect only because of this added coupon bonus.

The floor was strewn with discarded feed sacks (with the coupons torn off) and dried clumps of mud and dirt along with various other debris that accumulated over the years. The south-facing exterior of this remarkable old building was used as a drying rack. It was imprinted with numerous grease-stained circles where Dad had stretched and nailed freshly skinned beaver and raccoon pelts to allow them to dry in the winter sun.

On the other side of this building was nothing but a large bin for the cobs used to fuel our kitchen stove. They were scooped off the wagon by my dad and into the cob shed through a large door that hinged down and latched at the top. This is where they were stored until winter for use in the nonelectric side of the kitchen stove.

The cob barrel was painted silver and sat next to the stove in the kitchen. Rust showed through where the paint was chipped or scraped off. Someone in the past had painted the barrel in an effort to make it look like something other than what it really was—a cut-in-half fifty-five-gallon oil drum. The top edge was rather sharp where it had been hacksawed off.

Nevertheless, it worked, and this is where I dumped the cobs, and an occasional mouse I hauled from the shed with a faded red-rimmed wood-staved bushel basket left over from the apples Mom bought at DeGroot's Orchard. It was my responsibility to make sure the cob barrel did not become empty.

To fill the basket I was sternly told to use an old seven-tine pitchfork with two tines missing and three bent from getting it too hot while being used to back burn the area around the shuck pile before setting it on fire. This was like eating melted ice cream with a fork: not very efficient.

One day I decided to use Dad's new #14 aluminum scoop shovel, which I snuck out of the granary to fill the basket. It was an absolute dream come true. I had that basket full with three shovelfuls.

I would soon discover the problem. When filling the basket with the old fork, the chaff, which was mixed in with the cobs through the shelling process, would sift down through the tines and fall back onto the floor. When using the shovel, I scooped an inordinate amount of chaff into the basket along with the cobs.

Since I had previously been using the fork, there was a great deal of chaff on the floor, and it was all in with that basket of cobs soon to be delivered to the kitchen.

Upon entering the kitchen, like always, I dumped the basket of cobs into that cob barrel with one huge poof. Low and behold, a huge puff of chaff and dust formed a small mushroom cloud that spread not only throughout the kitchen but through every open door leading to it. Not good! This was definitely a "Lonny Joe, what-are-you-thinking moment."

Now why would anyone suspect that an eight-year-old boy possesses the ability to think—at least that far anyway? I suppose the dust finally did settle, I don't remember. I only remember the horror on Mom's face as she came running into the kitchen where the dust and chaff were settling everywhere as they flickered in the sunlight streaming through the long windows on the east kitchen wall.

Yikes! Invention for this kid definitely took a couple steps backward that day. I never used the scoop to fill the basket again.

The south storm door on our old porch was held shut with a latch that required me to pull on the handle to open it.

One very cold day while hauling the cobs to the kitchen (after scooping them with the pitchfork; I only had to learn that lesson once), it dawned on me that it would be much more efficient to pull on the latch with my teeth instead of putting the basket of cobs on the ground, opening the door in a normal manner, and picking up the basket again. As my lips enveloped the handle, of course they froze tight, and as I screamed for help, my tongue froze to the handle as well.

There I was with a bushel basket of cobs that I couldn't put down and I didn't want to drop for fear of spilling them into the snow, with my mouth frozen to the door handle, screaming through my nose for help. At the moment I thought I could no longer hang onto the basket, the heat from my body warmed the handle enough to release my lips and tongue with my skin mostly intact.

Here is the lesson: Efficiency is good. However be sure you have considered all the steps and their consequences before proceeding. And if that is too much to remember, just keep your mouth closed when confronting a metal object in the dead of a Nebraska winter.

7

WILD WEEDS, LUSH LIFE

When I was about seven, my dad fabricated a power mower using a discarded washing machine engine, some scrap iron, and three bright red eight-inch wheels retrieved from a crinkled cardboard box of junk brought home from a farm auction. The drive system included two recycled pulleys and a used water pump belt.

He went to all this work welding the pieces together and setting up the engine so it would drive the blade made from a leaf spring from an old car. I remember well the first time he tried it and discovered it required much more power to operate a weed mower than it did to power a washing machine. The whole contraption was retired to a weed patch behind the tool shop and remained there for two decades or more.

I wish I could retrieve that home-built mower. My dad must have wanted our farmyard to be a little neater. If not, he would not have gone to the trouble of building a mower. He must have been truly disappointed in its failure.

Growing up on the farm and watching my dad, I learned again and again that if you wait until you have all that is required to be successful, you likely never will be. It is possible to build something with junk. You see, that mower did in fact run. It simply did not have enough power. I can only assume that he thought he failed. However, I am absolutely sure that experience affected my thinking.

That may have been the day our company Weiland Doors came into existence in the mind of a little boy who was watching and learning. I thank my dad for that. If he hadn't tried, maybe I wouldn't have either.

Several years later, maybe when I was about eleven, my dad returned from a farm sale with a used lawn mower. It was about a 1950 model, self-propelled Moz-All with a four-horsepower Briggs and Stratton engine. By the time we got it, the muffler was rusted completely away, the drive cogs were nearly worn smooth, and the safety shield around the

Replica of first lawnmower with blade guard installed.

blade was missing. That machine was a safety inspector's nightmare. However, it did mow weeds very efficiently.

This was the first real lawnmower we ever owned. The weeds around our house were atrociously high and messy, but my dad didn't seem to care. But he became defensive whenever the issue was mentioned; so maybe he did care but was embarrassed to talk about it. After all, he did buy a mower.

One day when he was off on a corn-shelling job, I decided to mow the grass and weeds along our driveway. I mowed all day and got about half the weeds mowed when my father came home. He just took one look at what I had done and was disgusted. He angrily criticized me for attempting to wear out his "new" mower. All I wanted was to have our place look like Bill and Mable Mazuch's across the road.

I never did that again. I waited until I had my own place. I then bought a mower of my own, and by the way I wore that sucker out and several since. I think Jean and I now have one of the more beautiful farms in Madison County.

Here is the lesson: You can deprive your children of anything you wish while they are children. But when they are adults, they will likely acquire whatever you have deprived them of. So be careful. If you deprive them basics such as love and attention, they may try to get it from anyone who will give it to them—even at the price of their own soul.

8

THE MOST EFFECTIVE TEACHER

My dad was always busy; he rarely sat around idle. He simply did not understand the idea of laziness. In the winter when there wasn't any fieldwork to do, he'd trap muskrats, beavers, raccoons, and, once in a great while, a mink. That was always a good day because mink pelts brought the most money. He loved to trap. He'd get up in the morning, do the animal chores, and spend the rest of the day on his trap line. At night, he'd skin whatever he had caught in his traps.

The east upstairs room in our house was used as a processing area. After the skins were removed from the animals, they would be stretched over a drying frame with the flesh side out. Dad had a hundred or more of these frames of various sizes fabricated from cedar shingles. Since the largest pelts returned the most money, Dad would stretch them over the largest frame on which they would fit.

After they dried, any flesh that remained on the fur was removed by scraping with a skinning knife. I was taught to do this scraping job at a young age. Later I learned to remove the skin from the animals as well. If the skinning was done correctly, the pelt would have no cuts and very little flesh remaining. A cut in the pelt would decrease its value. Any flesh on the pelt would need to be removed later so it could completely dry.

My dad only trapped along creek banks. He always placed his traps so the animal, upon being caught, would instinctively dive into the stream and drown because the weight of the steel trap would not allow it to surface for air. All of his traps were modified with extra-long stake chains to allow the animal to get to the deepest part of the stream. In the wild most all animals die by disease or predators. Either way would be a whole lot more painful way to die than drowning in one of my father's traps.

The money he earned from selling his furs was added to our family income. He proudly made a cash purchase of that 1954 International pickup truck with money he earned from selling furs. This was the first truck he ever owned. Many farmers at that time did not have a truck. He was extremely proud of it.

When that old truck was about ten years old, I was given the responsibility of feeding some hogs at another farmyard about a mile from our house. My dad allowed me to drive there. This was a basic truck—nothing like the plush units sold today with everything from power brakes to navigation systems. This was a one-ton unit with a four-speed on the floor, a heater, bench seat, and a steering wheel.

By the time I drove it, the taillights were busted out and the turn signals didn't work. The seat was worn out with sagging springs showing through the alligator-cracked brown plastic upholstery.

As a runty adolescent, I could barely see out the side windows or over the dash. While I drove I had to crane my neck to look through the steering wheel to see where I was going.

I'm telling you, I just loved to do the hog chores on the other farm. I was king while driving that old pickup truck!

Here is the lesson: I believe many parents are concerned about giving their children too many chores, about making them work too hard. It seems to me that there is no way of determining exactly how much work is necessary to teach a child to be most productive when he or she becomes an adult. An error on this point is bound to occur. So that being the case, it would seem, to me anyway, that it would be better to err on the too-much-work side. I have yet to know of a child who gained a sense of accomplishment from too much time on a PlayStation, although I have seen the opposite. It seems that many parents are training their children to grow up to be children. What an absurdity. Is it not a fact that most people spend three times as much of their lives being physically mature adults? So if you are one of those lenient parents, get some guts. It's not easy, but if you don't do it, who will? It's your job!

My father used the corn sheller he owned not only to shell the corn we raised on our farm, but also to do custom work for other area farmers who did not own one. There were many weeks when this machine was busy every single day, except Sunday, of course.

Sometime around the time I was ten years old, my dad decided I was old enough to grease (lubricate the moving parts) the sheller. As I would climb around on the machine applying grease to the various fittings, my skin and clothing gathered a mixture of dirt, grease, and corn chaff. It was a dirty job, to say the least.

In helping my dad, I gathered an understanding of the working parts of that machine, but I also learned about my dad's day-to-day work.

My dad's daily tasks were incessant. He was never idle. At two different times while I was a youngster my dad bought an old abandoned farmhouse and salvaged the lumber to build various things on our farm. I remember him saying, "If you gotta buy the lumber, you're never going to build anything."

It was my job to remove the nails from the lumber after Dad disengaged it from the old structure. This was a horribly boring job for a daydreaming youngster such as me. All day long, with an old wooden-handled claw hammer, I pulled the nails from the boards and put them into an old tin pail to be straightened and reused later. I stacked the lumber in a straight pile on the ground.

Later Dad loaded it into his pickup and hauled it back to our farm where it was stored on the north half of the barn.

The salvaged lumber and nails were used to make an ample supply of livestock gates. The short pieces formed the bridge across the corners of the farrowing pens to prevent the sows from pinning the little pigs against the fence, thereby suffocating them. The landlord owned the buildings. However the farrowing pens were constructed mostly from the lumber gleaned from salvaged buildings. Dad thought it important to construct his own pens because the way they were constructed was vital to preventing the baby pigs from being stepped on and crushed by the sows.

I don't recall any of the lumber being used to repair any of our buildings. After all, those buildings belonged to the landlord. I doubt that my father's line of thinking would have allowed him to use material gained with his personal sweat to repair the property of someone who already owned the farm.

As I watched my dad be industrious with the little he had, I'm sure that experience had an effect on me later in life. Some of the lessons I learned from him went without realization until I wrote this book. The self-sufficiency and personal toughness I learned from him has benefited my family and me in ways I am sure we still do not realize.

One time when I was a teenager standing in the bathroom waiting for him to finish washing up for lunch, I was complaining about something long forgotten. He turned to me and, in an absolute tone of voice, said, "When you're a man, you have to decide what needs to be done and then do it." There was no hesitancy in his voice. I knew exactly what he meant.

I still remember the incident. No questions need to be asked. I was expected to act like a man. Anything else would not be tolerated.

Alfalfa harvest or "putting up hay," as we called it, was a nonstop summer farm activity when I was young and living at home.

When I got to be about fourteen, my dad thought it no longer necessary to hire an extra man to help with the hay harvest. I was old enough.

We had a sickle mower with a manual lift mounted on a 1936 John Deere Model "A." Weathered, slivery boards had long before replaced the cushioned seat that once softened the bumps for some young farmer luckier than I. Much of the paint was gone, along with the muffler that had once quieted the "POP, POP, POP" of the engine. Steam continuously

Old green tractor

hissed out around where the gasket was missing on the top of a radiator, which required filling with water every time the gas tank was topped off.

But the most difficult thing about that old tractor (which, by the way, I still own) was the manual lift for the sickle bar. This is the part of the mower that sticks out the side that severs the alfalfa stalk from the root. The severed plants would invariably bunch up and plug the sickle. This would require me—a kid who weighed less than a hundred pounds—to stop the tractor, back my butt up against the front of the seat, and with all my might push the foot-controlled lift lever down and forward to lift the sickle off the ground in order to unplug it. That was hard for me as a boy. But I wasn't. I was a man, and I was expected to act like one.

In those days men were men, period. I'm proud to have grown up knowing that.

On our farm my mother or my sisters rarely worked in the field. It was primarily a man's job to provide for his family. If a wife wants to add to the family's income, I think that is wonderful. However, I think if she chooses to be a homemaker, that should be her choice, and if a man has to work two jobs to provide, then that is his responsibility.

All too often I hear of women who work their forty hours and come home to another forty hours of housework while the "man" sits in his easy chair watching football on TV. As if that has anything to do with being a man.

Here is the lesson: Men should be gentle and kind when dealing with personal needs of their families. Outside of that they should be tenacious individuals who get out there and fight whatever battle there is to provide for their families and, by doing so, teach their sons to do the same ... and teach their daughters how real men act and to be satisfied with nothing less.

As a teenager I was constantly jumping over whatever was in my way. It didn't matter if it was a fence, the creek in the pasture, or a manure pile. If I thought I could hurdle it, I'd give it a shot.

One cold January morning when I was fifteen or so, I was on my way to feed our sheep, which was another one of my responsibilities as a young man.

The time I allotted to my chores was somewhere between "lickity split" and "slower than a seven-year itch." Some days I did my chores quickly and some days at a snail's pace. The speed at which I worked was usually dependent on the amount of daydreaming I was doing at the time, which usually depended whether or not Dad was off shelling corn somewhere. My pace varied so much, only one thing was certain: you could never set your watch by my work habits.

That particular winter morning I'd taken off for the sheep pen in a dead run. The only thing separating me and the sheep was a dilapidated barbed-wire fence strung with wool from animals satisfying an itch now and then. As I approached the fence, instead of slowing to a walk, I hurdled it in a way that would put any high school athlete to shame.

What happened next was a blur. A second later I was lying on a layer of frozen sheep manure.

Now if you happen to be familiar with frozen sheep poop, you're probably aware that it's in the shape of cat-eye marbles and just as hard.

You can imagine how I looked sprawled on the ground amid several startled black-face, woolly ewes, with marble-sized indentations on the part of my body that had just a moment prior violently contacted the frozen ground.

As I sat up to regain my composure, I turned and there he was. Glaring green eyes. Nostrils flaring. Ears back as if pasted against his black head, charging straight toward me. Bang! That old buck sheep nailed me in the side of the head with a concerted blow that sent me reeling back to the frozen ground. He had allowed me no time to recover from the self-administered blow seconds earlier. The only thing in that pen harder than the frozen manure was that buck sheep's head.

The pain was excruciating while the stars in my head were numerous. This time, though, I stayed prone on the ground until he walked off knowing he had eliminated any threat I may have posed to his numerous girlfriends.

When I did finally come around, I realized that being knocked on my rear didn't mean I was immune to being knocked on my back if I made another dumb decision. A friend of mine from Texas tells me, "If you want to be dumb, you better be tough, and the dumber you are, the tougher you better get." I would add that if you want to butt heads with a sheep, be sure you have a thick skull. That sounds like reasonable advice to me.

Here is the lesson: Sh** can be an effective teacher from time to time. Don't ever forget that if you're stuck in it and praying to find a way out, staying in it for a while might be the answer to your prayers.

9

GRANDMA GOODWATER AND THE PEACH CRATE

My Grandma Goodwater was sixty-nine years old when I was born. My Grandpa Goodwater had died the year before I was born. She lived with my bachelor uncle, Albert, on a farm several miles northwest of Madison. I assume my uncle continued the farming operation after my grandfather passed on. It was a natural progression since he lived with my grandparents at the time.

Unlike our house, their house had paint all over. And out front was a huge weeping willow that swayed in the wind. Small broken branches always littered the ground under the massive tree. I helped Grandma pick up the branches every once in a while. On the back side of the house was a large elm tree that shaded the house and a stand of spearmint. When there was only a slight breeze, the aroma smelled like a pack of Wrigley's gum. During the summer petunias populated her flower garden unleashing a heavenly scent pervading the memory of at least one little boy.

Grandma raised chickens—several hundred to be sure. She had two chicken coops. The bigger one was for the laying hens. The walls of this building were lined with nesting boxes where the hens deposited their eggs. The

Leon, brother Gerry, sisters Dianne and Linda,
and Grandma Goodwater

nesting boxes were about ten inches wide by twelve high and fifteen inches deep with oat straw in the bottom. They were in rows as long as the wall and two to four rows high. Along each row was a poop-encrusted perch where the hen could leave the nest without jumping immediately to the floor. The other chicken house was where she raised the pullets before they began laying eggs.

My job when I would visit Grandma's was helping her pull the watering hose from one building to the other in order to fill the chicken waters. This was a novelty to me because at that time we did not yet have a pressured water system, which meant I hauled the water to our chickens in buckets.

By the time I recall any real connection with her, she was in her mid-seventies. Her skin was rather wrinkled, and her hands and forearms were soft and silky and smelled of Camay Beauty Soap. My memory of her is nothing less than soft and gentle. There was a frilly pink curtain suspended from a wooden rod across her bedroom door. On the wall just inside the door was a black, wall-mounted telephone with the numbers GL4-6683 stamped in the center of the dial. Also, just inside, was a vanity where she kept the good smelling things that made her smell like my grandma.

She made the absolute best homemade bread. When she baked it, the aroma filled her house. The crust on Grandma's bread was slightly over-baked, which I believe added to its distinct flavor.

To go along with the bread she always had real sweet cream butter on hand, unlike the margarine we always had at home. She always let me spread the butter as thick as I wanted. It was absolutely fabulous. The scent of freshly baked bread always takes me to my Grandma Goodwater's place.

In addition to having a reputation for making the most delicious goodies, she loved crafts. She always had an assortment of materials. It was one of those paradises that kids latch onto, with trinkets and artifacts that opened up an infinite world of imagination.

As a young boy in the 1950s, I never came in contact with new lumber. However, during the summer, farm women bought canning peaches to store for the winter. These peaches came in wooden crates that could be pried apart and used as materials to make other things.

Rosy peach crate

When I was about six or seven, my Grandma Goodwater helped me make a birdhouse using this recycled wood.

We cut the pieces with a hand saw and assembled it with the nails we retrieved when we disassembled the crate. We drilled a hole in the end for the birds to enter. Just below that we drove a sixteen-penny nail for them to perch before entering. When it was finished, we painted it green. I was very proud. This was the first item I can remember building, thanks to Grandma.

After that I was hooked. I discovered that peach crates were useful in building other things as well. The box for my first wheelbarrow was made from one of these peach crates. In addition, I also used several slats from a discarded section of wooden snow fence.

Farmers during that era used rings of wooden snow fence to form the exterior of a makeshift corn crib. When the

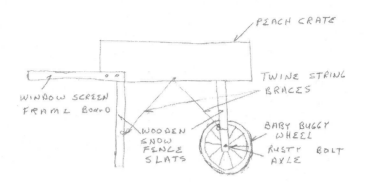

Sketch of first wheelbarrow

ring was filled with ear corn, another ring was constructed on top and a second layer was formed, and then a third or fourth in the same manner. Depending on the number of rings, it was called a two, three, or four-ring corn pile.

Three ring corn piles

In addition to the slats and peach crate, I salvaged a rusted, bent wheel from an old baby buggy I found in the junk pile along the road ditch bordering the east end of our farm. I then fashioned the whole thing together into a wheelbarrow using baler twine for bracing.

Of course the wheelbarrow didn't work. It sagged into a heap the first time I stood it upright.

Even though it didn't work, I learned how not to build the next one. The second wheelbarrow I built was somewhat more sophisticated. I constructed it with a couple two-by-twos from Dad's lumber pile and the sides of an old window screen. In addition to that, I used an old nail keg and an old tricycle wheel from my Uncle Arny.

That wheelbarrow actually worked. I used it to do my chores. I found an old cream bucket that fit near perfectly into the nail keg box. I used it to carry water and grain to

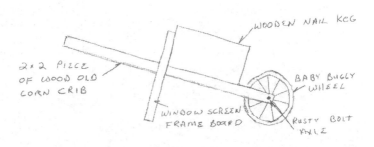

Sketch of wheelbarrow

feed the chickens. I always filled it with grain first because putting grain in a wet bucket caused grain to stick to the bottom and sides.

Nevertheless, I discovered the satisfaction of creating a useful tool. On a good night, with the use of that wheelbarrow, I could feed and water the chickens in five minutes. On other nights it might take two hours. On those other nights I was more than likely caught up in a daydream imagining some other item to make.

I was always building something. When I was ten years old on a visit to Grandma Goodwater's house, I discovered a broken-down gasoline-powered washing machine engine in the back corner of her wash house. These engines had been replaced with electric motors after the rural electrification. I learned why when I got this contraption home and tried to start it.

Washing machine engine

The foot pedal engaged a gear attached to the flywheel. In order to start the engine, one simply needed to close the choke and pump on the pedal—or so I thought. After hours of doing this it became apparent my efforts were futile. It simply refused to start.

Our neighbor, Homer Anderson, loved to tinker with small engines. So the next time he came by, I asked him to check my engine over. He simply screwed out the spark plug, poured a little gasoline into the hole, replaced the plug, and two pumps later it was running like a song—and what a song to my ears it was. This little operation is called priming the engine. I have used this lesson time after time since.

Of course my little victory only led to another problem and that was what to do with a running washing machine engine. Somewhere I had seen a gasoline engine power a machine simply by using friction between a bushing fastened to the motor shaft and a rubber-covered wheel. Why wouldn't this same idea work to power the back wheel of a bicycle?

When my dad had gone shelling corn, I sneaked into the tool shed to rummage through his scrap iron supply, trying to find just the right pieces of iron. I was looking for something I could weld to the bicycle frame onto which I could attach the washing machine engine. I refer to it as "the bicycle" because it was the only one we had.

My dad's shop, just like the rest of his farm, was in disarray. He rarely threw anything away. His workbench was covered with bolts, nuts, gears, levers, empty boxes, recycled Prince Albert cans of rivets, and Butternut

Coffee cans full of nails along with various pieces of you-name-it, it was there. There was rarely a bare spot on which to put anything else.

On one end of the bench were some vertical cupboards filled with all the owner's manuals for every piece of equipment my dad ever owned. Just below the cupboards was an opening bordered on one side by a dilapidated door panel, which hung precariously by only the top hinge. Inside the opening was a collection of small odds and ends of salvaged steel machine parts gleaned from obsolete farm machinery, which once tilled the Nebraska soil. Most of it was cast iron, which was difficult to weld.

I rarely found anything useful in there. But whenever I wanted to build something, I'd sift through that pile, hoping to miraculously find a piece I could use.

That day was no different. I scoured Dad's shop looking for the right piece of discarded material to put my idea into action. To my surprise, I found a bent, rusty, eight-inch barn door hinge. This was as perfect as perfect ever got.

Using the welder opened up a whole new world for me as a boy. I had watched Dad weld pieces of steel together looking through the welding helmet that came with the welder after Dad bought a better one at a farm sale. He explained how the trick was to select the correct heat setting along with keeping the welding electrode moving fast enough so as not to burn through the metal, yet slow enough to melt the two pieces of steel together.

Once again I was hooked. Not only could I nail together pieces of wood, I could weld pieces of steel.

After hammering the hinge straight over a giant anvil that was perched on a sawed-off piece of tree stump amid an array of items of questionable value strewn across the floor, I welded the hinge to the rear wheel fork of the bicycle, just below the seat and above the back tire. After drilling a couple holes in precise locations, I was able to mount the washing machine engine onto the hinge. The pulley mounted on the engine shaft rested on the tire.

I mounted the bicycle and began pedaling. To my amazement, the engine fired up and off I went.

It would do ten miles per hour on level ground, fourteen or fifteen downhill; going uphill required pedaling because the engine was not powerful enough to do that much work.

I always wanted to keep my homemade contraptions hidden from my dad for fear of what'd he say about them. But he couldn't have been so oblivious to not notice what I was doing. Maybe he actually had a soft spot for the playfulness of youth.

Another time I built a wooden go-cart. I took the engine off the bicycle and mounted it on what I thought was a beautiful wooden go-cart. However I had no way of connecting the engine to the drive wheel. So I just used the go-cart as a place to sit and daydream.

I do not recall whatever happened to it. I remember it being in the same spot by the chicken coop behind our house for several years while I became interested in other building projects.

When I was young, I had a set of red plastic building blocks—the small set because the large sets were expensive. It was a set that only allowed me to build one style of house. I built that house dozens and dozens of times.

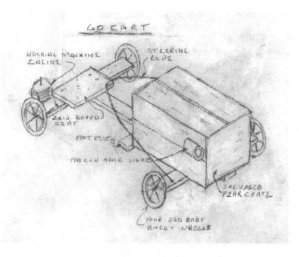

My wooden go-cart

Before moving to the farm where I grew up, my mom and dad had lived on a farm northwest of Madison across the road from Elmer and Ruth Schmidt and a half mile west of the farm place where my dad's sister Shirley and her husband Ralph Wolken raised a family of six boys. After we moved, we visited the Schmidts a couple times. Their son Melvin had the most fabulous set of building blocks I had ever seen. They were probably the predecessors to Legos. Melvin could build anything he wanted with those blocks and still have some left over when he was finished. I wanted a set of building blocks like it, but I never got one.

The same was true when I requested an erector set with an electric motor. An erector set consisted of a variety of small steel pieces along with nuts and machine screws that could be fastened together to make all sorts of things. My brother Gerry received one for Christmas several years later, which I used and used until I had built about everything imaginable. The little electric motor didn't have as much power as I had hoped, but I still had hours and hours of fun. I just loved building things.

I found that set with the old toys in Mom and Dad's attic. When we threw some of the old toys away after Dad passed away and Mom was confined to a nursing home, Gerry said that set was mine. I think he thought that because I was the only one who used it. Anyway it is now in my attic collecting dust.

Because I didn't have many toys growing up, I was forced to find other ways of entertaining myself. When I wasn't taking make-believe trips to California in a rusted out truck body sitting on apple crates or constructing wheelbarrows out of peach crates, I'd go fishing.

Union Creek was within a quarter mile of our house in the middle of a cow pasture. Since the land along the creek had a propensity to flood, it wasn't deemed suitable for farming, so most farmers used the area as pasture for their cattle. Because Union Creek ran through the middle of cow pasture, most of the tall weeds and grass that usually sprout up along streams in Nebraska were trampled down or eaten, making the creek easily accessible.

There was more than one way to fish. For one, I had an old cane pole with a piece of kite string and a real hook that I swiped from Dad's tackle box. I used a 3/8-inch threaded nut from Dad's bolt bin as a sinker and found something that would float to use as a bobber. My bait was fat juicy earthworms, hand dug out of the dirt in the cow yard behind our house.

Several times on really hot summer days, I'd strip down to my underwear and wade right into the water. On days when the water was warm and the carp were lazy, I moved slowly along the bank or brush piles until I felt the twitch of a carp's tail. After feeling my way around to determines the exact location of the fish, I'd pounce on it, pushing it down into the mud. I'd then grab its tail with one hand and put the index finger of my other hand in its mouth, while placing my thumb in its gill and then pull it out of the water. The carp lost its life because it was lazy and not paying attention.

I learned this from my dad. There were many things he enjoyed that cost little or nothing. Before the advent of swimming pools, the creek was a cool way to spend a hot Sunday afternoon.

As I was usually fabricating some sort of contraption or other, I learned that fish could also be caught with a fish trap constructed from sections of bent, discarded electric fence posts and some chicken wire I found in the grove west of the chicken coop. I welded a cylindrical-shaped frame from the fence posts and wrapped it with the chicken wire, leaving a recessed hole in the ends large enough for fish to enter. Once the fish entered the trap, they'd swim back and forth along the sides of the trap, unable to find a way out.

This was a sure way to catch fish. I guess that was why it was illegal—something my dad taught me to pay little attention to as long as the fish were Friday's dinner.

Over the years, I've found that much of my outlook on life is grounded in the way I work with my hands. My farmhouse, for example, has been an ongoing "work in progress" since we purchased it along with the 250-acre adjoining farm in

Leon and Jean's farm home in Madison, Nebraska

1987—after having lived there the previous twelve years as a tenant. I've always been in the process of some sort of beautification project around our farm.

When we purchased it, there were three smaller porches attached on three sides. The wood was rotted where they were fastened to the main body of the structure, so I removed them while salvaging the spindle-style support posts. Later, using those same posts, I constructed a new porch across the entire front of the house styled after a picture I had of our home not long after it was built.

A year after the purchase I constructed a beautiful first-floor deck with a swimming pool in the center, which has given countless hours of enjoyment to our friends and family over the years. Inside I have completely rebuilt everything according to its original Victorian style.

When we bought the place, it definitely needed a facelift inside and out. That's one reason I have spent so much effort in building. But the other reason I've spent so much time working on our home and farm over the years is the joy I get from confronting a problem hands-on.

Working with my hands has always been an outlet of thought for me. It's allowed me to direct my energy into something concrete, something tangible. I like to be able to touch whatever it is on which I am working and, in doing so, obtain not only a deeper understanding of what I'm really holding, but a cosmic understanding that circumvents the small stuff that so often gets in the way significant thought.

Here is the lesson: Feel and touch. This is what makes reality. Do something with your hands. Build a birdhouse, play the piano, make a paper airplane, hug your family. It makes no difference. There is something about feeling and touching that unifies and connects you to all that is.

10

THE CHURCH: MY FAITH FOUNDATION

My memory of Catholic ritual is colorfully vivid. The sound of Latin chants, the pungent smell of incense, and liturgical celebration, all part of a two-thousand-year tradition, are a part of my spiritual identity.

We were a devout Catholic family, and my parents made sure we were raised in a home of faith. We attended St. Leonard's Catholic Church in Madison. It's the same church where Jean and I raised our children and the same church we attend today.

Constructed shortly after the turn of the twentieth century, St. Leonard's is known for its large clock tower that is atop the rounded arch entryway which is visible to drivers on nearby Highway 81.

Church life was a very important part of my family as a child. We routinely attended weekly Mass and Reconciliation, along with all the ritual events throughout the church year. Those experiences, in conjunction with my Catholic grade school education, were instrumental in my faith development. Seeing my parents' example, although not fully understood as a boy, brought firsthand to life what I was taught in Catholic grade school. The formal education and what I saw at home fit together well.

What I remember most about my early days in St. Leonard's is the code of conduct my siblings and I were expected to follow. Church was the place for my parents to enforce their rules and make sure we behaved. I think this special attention along with the formidable presence of God's hand made for better results than my parents saw at home.

My dad always said, "If you don't sit still in church, I'll make sure you sit still when we get home." And he wasn't kidding. On the few occasions that I didn't behave myself in church, I was forced to sit on the couch absolutely still for what seemed like hours; however, I doubt it was ever longer than fifteen minutes.

We were expected to be quiet in church. Because of the fabulous acoustics in that building, the sounds of little voices and the bumping of shoes on the pew were magnified several times for all to hear. It was a little boy's dream and, at the same time, his nightmare. My dad would have to have been as deaf as my great uncle George not to notice. My grandfather Weiland's brother George read lips because he was stone deaf. Nothing, it seemed, got past my father's scrutiny.

For Christmas when I was eight years old, I received a cowboy outfit that included a pair of Roy Rogers cowboy boots—black on the bottom and turquoise on the top. They were so cool. I wore them everywhere.

One day as I was rummaging through some clutter in the attic, I came across a shoe repair kit that included some heel cleats, a shoe repair anvil, nails, and a small hammer. What a find!

During the fifties, it was in vogue for high school boys to attach half-moon-shaped steel cleats such as these to their shoe heels. This caused a "click-clack" sound as they walked. Using the tools in the shoe repair kit, I attached these to the heels of my boots. Whether or not my parents realized what I had done, I do not know, but they were about to find out.

That Sunday, because I invariably didn't remember to go before we left for church, I had to use the bathroom in the church basement. As I walked down the aisle toward the back of church, I made no effort to quiet the clicking sound of those cleats against the cold, hard green-and-black tile church floor. It must have echoed to every silent corner of that giant building. Every adult in Mass that Sunday fixed a glance on me as I walked down the aisle.

For a moment I was the center of attention. No doubt Mom and Dad were absolutely mortified. It was not a good time after church that day. I remember removing the metal cleats from my boots and after that walking on my tiptoes in church just for good measure. In church we were supposed to be quiet.

Being in church wasn't all bad, though. I found it easy to lose myself inside the warm confinement of St. Leonard's stained glass windows. The beauty of that church impressed me as a child. I remember being in awe as I sat and witnessed its elegance. It was highly ornate and still impresses me today. Even as a little boy I remember appreciating the beauty inside that church. The architecture, the altar, the paintings, the relics, the stained glass windows—all made an impression on me.

St. Leonard church
Madison, Nebraska

I spent a lot of time daydreaming during those visits to St. Leonard's, but I was also mesmerized by the rituals of the Mass celebration.

I attended St. Leonard grade school where, beginning in the first grade, I was taught the basic truths of the Catholic faith. I still recite the prayers I learned during this time in my life. This is where the Benedictine nuns taught me about the existence of the physical body of Christ. Today I am more convinced than ever of the truth of this doctrine.

As a youth in the fourth grade I became an altar server at Mass. In my training I was first required to memorize and recite the Latin prayers. After that I was taught the correct way of doing the necessary actions included in the service.

We learned to genuflect (one knee to the floor in recognition of the physical presence of Jesus) together and at the precise times while folding my hands in a prayerful way pointing up toward heaven. I learned to light the incense for Benediction and to quickly pop the candle lighter wick back out before the melted wax hardened and stuck it tight.

Ringing the chimes or bells at the Consecration was also a much anticipated part of serving at Mass. Being part of this amazing event most certainly has had a profound impact on my current love of Eucharistic Liturgy.

The physical existence of the body and blood of Jesus Christ under the appearance of bread and wine has been the central belief and tradition of the Catholic Church since it came into existence. This existence can be traced back to the time of Christ. I have found no reason not to believe this because I have no reason to doubt Jesus was the incarnation of the almighty and omnipotent God.

Some thirty years ago I regularly listened to a radio preacher who boastfully and enthusiastically stated at the beginning and end of his programs that "You have no troubles at all; all you need is faith in God." Really? We had four children to care for while low commodity prices and high interest rates had left us financially $100,000 in the red. A couple years later, after our son Carl was born, my wife, Jean, hemorrhaged so profusely, her pituitary gland was damaged leaving her chronically ill and weak.

We had faith in God; however, I was never convinced we had no problems at all. What I failed to understand at that time was that this program was a radio show, designed to retain listeners. Of course it had a feel-good message. That was part of the design. However that feel-good message had little in common with reality. Perhaps it was more like a drug designed to deaden the pain of our situation and little to do with solving the problem.

Traffic lights are used in virtually every country of the world to control automobile and pedestrian traffic. I doubt one could find much disagreement concerning their value in contributing to the safety and well-being of countless individuals. It is commonly understood that red means stop, green means go, and yellow means caution. Laws have been recorded to enable enforcement of this understanding. As long as everyone obeys the law, traffic proceeds rather smoothly.

On the other hand, what would be the case if there was no authority to enforce the law; or for that matter how might it be if there was no common understanding of what direction the traffic lights were giving? How long might it be before total chaos ensued? Can you even imagine? My guess is that in a short time the confusion caused by varying interpretations of this simple law along with rationalizations for ignoring this law would be as varied as religious beliefs in America.

For two thousand years the Catholic Church has retained spiritual authority and guarded the deposit of faith set forth in Christian tradition and the Holy Scriptures. During that time there have been no fundamental changes to its teaching. If not for the unchanging reality of the pilgrim church, by reason of evolution and democratization, how far might have religious faith come, diverted from where it is now? I find in the Catholic faith an extensive gathering together of faith and reason. I simply have not found this elsewhere. I find solace in this much like it might seem, that a baby finds it in the sides of its playpen. I know it isn't going to move or change.

Does this mean everything in the church is wonderful and clean? It sure isn't. Any given day you can read in the newspaper about human weakness among the members of the Catholic clergy. We have encountered gross sinfulness among its members, which will take generations to rectify. However, when I read these stories I ask myself if the writer's interest is in the truth as much as it is in his or her rationalization of his or her own shortcomings and in the unfortunate dismissal of all the good done by the vast majority of these individuals.

I had an incompetent priest as my pastor during the troubled early years of my life. In his ten years as pastor at St. Leonard's, I don't recall him undertaking even the repair of a window. And furthermore, he allowed a Protestant woman to be the head teacher in our Catholic school.

To top it all off, when I told him I was leaving the church, he simply shrugged his shoulders. I will never forget that day.

When he left, the parishioners bought him a car for a going-away gift. I thought that was only fitting for a guy who I thought should go a long, long way before he stopped. He smiled at everybody and provided leadership to no one.

In addition to this guy, when Jean and I were engaged to be married, the assistant pastor at the Catholic Church ignored the church rule that we were to receive premarital counseling. Because he was one of those progressive young priests coming out of the seminary in those days, he was soft on the foundational doctrines of the church such as contraception. I do not remember the cockamamie reasoning he gave for his thinking, but it was absolutely counter to everything the Catholic Church teaches on this subject. Furthermore the absence of premarital counseling had a devastating effect on our early marriage.

The first of these fellows was one of those lazy priests who did nothing to merit being fired, but was a wet noodle of a man and did spiritual damage every day he walked out of his house. The second of these guys was just flat out incompetent. It seems to me if the Roman Catholic Church did not have the hand of God guiding it, knuckleheads like these would have buried it centuries ago.

My brother-in-law, Leon Haschke, once stated jokingly that he thought it was possible the bishop calculated where some of these guys would do the least amount of damage when assigning them to a parish. It is a godsend to the church that the qualifications for allowing young men into the seminary are more stringent than they had been for the last forty years of the twentieth century.

On the other hand Father James Ryberg came to St. Leonard's during the time I was exploring other faiths. As a man's man, Father Ryberg was a godsend to me. He engaged me in my faith unlike any other priest ever had. At the heart of it, he was a teacher. On Sunday mornings his sermons were direct and engaging. This didn't always agree with other parishioners who were used to the previous ten years of canned sermons designed to hurt no one's feelings.

He taught about the Catholic Church in a way that I could understand. His homilies caught my attention. They grabbed and tugged at my innermost questions and forced me to examine my commitment to the Catholic faith. It wasn't a theology of mush; it was sound thinking. And at the time, I needed something in my life that made sense.

I remember visiting with him after Mass one Sunday to discuss my thoughts on his homily and the teachings of the day's readings. It was that day he pointed out to me the difference between fundamentalism and Catholicism. He showed me the feel-good message being preached in many churches doesn't always fix real-life problems. But instead they are more like a drug to dull the pain. Through much observation I have come to believe that to be close to the truth.

That was the type of man he was. Just like his faith and his delivery, Father Ryberg was rock solid. He not only gave me a strong faith background, which was logical and sensible, he became a good friend. His positive influence on my life was paramount in unraveling the damage done by "priests of the little boys club" who lack the spiritual balls to put the truth on the table and let the chips fall where they may.

However just as dirty windows do not affect the warmth inside, a few lazy and sinful priests do not affect the truth, warmth, and love that can be found inside the Catholic Church. Thousands of Catholic priests are serious in their vocation; they unfailingly demonstrate the love of God to their parishioners day in and day out.

I have been a member of St. Leonard Church for almost all of my sixty years. My walk with God has had hills and valleys, to say the least. I have to say, though, I love it here. This is where I have found the truth. In this faith community is where I experience the love of Jesus.

Here is the lesson: I believe one of the great sins of the world today is trying to make Jesus someone He is not. Just as the people during his human existence wanted to make Him an earthly king who would provide them food for their stomachs, I believe there are numerous churches abandoning what has always been considered the truth in order to grasp concepts that merely resonate in our hedonistic, individualistic American culture. Be careful. Truth doesn't change in order to accommodate public opinion.

11

MEETING JEAN

After high school, I enrolled at Norfolk Junior College in Norfolk, Nebraska, with the intention of studying psychology. Even though that never quite panned out, it wasn't due to a lack of intelligence, or the difficulty of the subject matter. As a student I was constantly distracted. There were a multitude of subjects I found interesting, most of which had no course name or written prospectus.

I was then and always have been a student of life—of the colorful, multifaceted events that compile a lifetime of experience. I had friends who could sit for hours studying a prescribed course. Even though to this day I wish I had a piece of paper that proclaims my intelligence and trainability, I doubt I have the focus to acquire one.

I have vowed to write this book and leave The Study of Neuroethology (word coined by me) to someone more suitable.

The life course in which I was probably most interested at that time in my life was simply called "girls." I liked girls. Prior to that time I had dated many, some sharp and interesting, some dull and boring. None of them seemed to be a match. That was about to change.

Here is a lesson: My upbringing taught me to be respectful to the opposite sex. I believed then, as I do now, that sexuality was a gift from God, that it was to be reserved for the one person with whom I would marry. Trust is fragile. It would seem that someone who would sleep with someone else's spouse, whether present or future, should never be completely trusted. For all who buy into the popular thinking that it is okay to have sex with anyone as long as they are not married, you are violating the trust, either yours or that of their future husband or wife.

One evening in the fall of 1969 as I was walking out of the Norfolk Junior College gym, my friend, John Brandl, parked his brown 1963, four-door Chevy Biscayne right in front of the building. By his side was what looked to me to be the most beautiful girl on whom I had ever laid these farm-boy eyes. The next thing I remember, I was sitting next to this beautiful young woman with water splashed all over me as a result of not noticing the water puddle next to the curb when I ran around the rear of his car.

That was an awkward beginning if there ever was one. I introduced myself and talked fast. I was definitely starting out in the hole this time, but I was an optimist. This little setback did not douse my hopes of getting to know this strikingly gorgeous young lady.

After some small talk we ended the meeting. I don't know what I did the rest of the evening other than dream!

After that I couldn't get my mind off her. I knew her name but I didn't know her address, phone number, or hometown. I assumed she may have been from Humphrey, a small town about ten miles south of Madison.

One Saturday night, a friend of mine and I drove all over Norfolk and Humphrey trying to meet up with her "coincidentally," if you could call it that. We never found her.

I didn't have the nerve to ask John Brandl. He might have slugged me, and that wasn't the greatest prospect to consider.

I was out of luck, so it seemed. I didn't know how to find her.

And then a couple months later I was in the school library, and there she was in a blue skirt with a matching blouse, no hose, hair undone, looking absolutely awful, as she later described herself. I was so elated, I didn't notice. It turned out she was there visiting a high school classmate who was dating my cousin. I learned how to contact her and shortly thereafter I asked her for a date.

On February 26, 1970, I had the first date with Jean. We went to watch a basketball game in Norfolk. She wore a brown tweed skirt with a matching vest over a brown silk blouse with matching brown shoes. In other words, she was impeccably dressed. I thought then as I do now that she was absolutely beautiful. It seems to me, sometimes, somewhat odd that I have never forgotten that night.

It became clear to me that I was head over heels for Jean. She was everything a young man could hope to find in a girl: beautiful, honest, independent, and comforting. I asked her several times for a second date, but it never seemed to work out. I even resorted to writing her a letter asking for another date, which brings me back to St. Leonard's.

I was doing some work in the basement of St. Leonard's, helping with the removal of the boiler and pouring concrete in its place, when I received a reply to my letter, which she had written on a piece of Mickey Mouse stationery. After she told me all she had been doing, she ended the letter by saying she was busy and "feel free to ask another."

Feel free to ask another? My heart sunk. I was head over heels for this girl and it's my experience that it's impossible to be crazy for one girl and ask another for a date at the same time. That just doesn't work.

So I began chasing after Jean. I was relentless. Over the next couple months I asked her out several times before she finally relented.

Later I found her reluctance stemmed from the fact that I was a year younger than her. That was a relief. I thought I was just annoying. Anyway, we were off.

It's fair to say that I had a good feeling about Jean as soon as we met. She was living in Norfolk at the time with an elderly woman called Mrs. Kluge. Living there gave the lady companionship and it made rent less expensive for Jean.

On the night of our first date, after we'd gotten back from the basketball game, Jean and I sat outside her house, talking. She told me all about herself, including a story about helping her brothers on the farm and something about electric fences and cows. I don't remember the details of her story, but I remember thinking to myself, *here's a genuinely neat person.*

Jean had the most refreshing personality I'd ever encountered. She was who she was and she was comfortable in her own skin. She didn't try to put on a front to impress people or give them a false sense of her identity. With Jean, what you saw was what you got, and she's still that way today.

Jean tells it like it is. She's an incredibly genuine person, and as lovely today as ever. That exuberant young girl I encountered in front of the college gym so many years ago is the same woman I'm married to today.

While I was in high school, my mother gave me a holy card. On the front of it was a picture of St. Joseph, my patron saint, and on the back a prayer asking God to bless me with the perfect mate. I think my prayer was answered by being blessed with the most incompatible person I could have imagined, yet the one who would help me be the man He wanted me to be.

Jean and I are true opposites, yet I believe us to be soul mates.

When I was a boy, we had a team of horses, Mike and Zip. Mike was white with some brown spots and very docile. On the other hand, Zip was dark brown and high spirited.

In the fall after the corn was harvested, there were always some corn ears on the ground that had fallen before the corn picking machine harvested the corn or that had escaped from the picker. Dad would hitch this unlikely team to a barge wagon and out to the field we'd go, Dad driving the horses and me riding along in the front corner of the wagon. Once in the field we'd walk beside the wagon, picking up the corn ears and throwing them up into the wagon.

When Dad wanted the wagon to move forward, he'd holler "Gee-Haw," and the horses would pull ahead until Dad would holler, "Whoa!"

What was interesting about Mike and Zip was how different they were. Mike would typically stand still while waiting to move the wagon forward while Zip was constantly sashaying back and forth, picking up and eating occasional prohibited ears of corn. He always wanted to go too fast and too far. Mike always had to hold him back. On the other hand Zip always made sure Mike didn't stop too soon or go too slow.

They were absolutely incompatible yet they made the perfect team. It seems to me many good marriages are that way as well. I think Jean and I are an example like that.

We were wed on February 12, 1972, at Holy Family Catholic Church in Jean's hometown of Lindsay, Nebraska. It was a beautiful ceremony, but nontraditional in every sense of the word.

Jean and I were never greatly influenced by the thoughts and opinions of others. This was probably evident in our wedding. For one, Jean didn't want her father to walk her down the aisle, claiming her father "didn't own her." Such independence wasn't necessarily a result of our indignation, but the time period in which we were married. Nevertheless, it didn't detract from the charm of the ceremony.

Jean wore a beautiful white dress. Which she had first seen in a bridal magazine. The bridesmaids all wore yellow dresses with orange trim.

I didn't wear a tuxedo, just a white gaucho shirt with puffy sleeves and white pants.

Our hair was long, in step with the styles of the era. In viewing our wedding photos, one would likely assess we were hippies of the time. I suppose in some sense we were.

A group of musicians from Norfolk played some lovely Christian folk music during the ceremony and at the reception. The highlight for me was walking down the aisle giving the sign of peace and seeing tears in the eyes of so many people. In typical Lindsay fashion, several hundred turned out for the event.

For the first years after we were married, I worked for a finance company, while Jean worked in retail clothing. During that time we resided in Omaha where we were introduced to city living. There was much about it that we liked. However we both liked the farm life even better.

We decided to go back to the farm and try to work with my dad. Returning home was also a dry run at seeing whether or not my father and I could get along if we worked side by side.

We had parted on bad terms when I left home for college. I remember that day well. He was putting up hay in the field east of the barn. I went out there to tell him goodbye. All he had to say to me were some guilt-ridden words, expressing his disappointment that I was leaving him to manage the farm himself.

Once we returned, the first few days of working with him on the farm went fine, but soon it became clear that our personalities didn't mesh as boss and employee. Try as we might, we just couldn't get along.

Everything on the farm was Dad's gig, and he had little tolerance for any concerns or desires I may have had. He was just plain abusive. Even then it seemed he would not allow me to work with him and be married to Jean at the same time. And even though I was trying desperately to gain his approval, one day I simply got tired and left … again. And again it was the guilt trip. Although this time I felt much less guilty.

From that disappointing experience I went to work for Jean's brother-in-law, Leon Haschke. In defiant contrast to my father's usual ranting, he had an unlimited supply of patience. He became my mentor and the key person in my life who offered me a vision of living without anger. While working with him, I noticed he rarely became upset. He'd occasionally find himself frustrated or stumped, but the result was never the lashing out type.

While working there I discovered a new way to earn a living, by the gig, not by the hour. He would buy corn from farmers at a premium price. We used his trucks to transport the grain from the farmer's bins to town, where we loaded it into railroad hopper cars and shipped it to where it needed to go, earning about 25 cents per bushel. This was about $1,200 per car; in 1973 that was a bunch of money.

He was constantly scheming over the possibility of another way of turning a buck. He converted these profits into leveraged purchases of farmland. The 1980s were a stressful time for farmers as they saw their financial well-being flush down the toilet as the value of their assets dropped by two-thirds. Caught it this vicious chain of events, Leon suffered a massive stroke in 1987, which left him debilitated and blind. Even through all that, I never once saw him lash out in anger. The value of what I learned from him was priceless.

He was one of my true heroes. In 2000 he passed away after thirteen years of therapy and nursing home care.

The positive experience of working with Leon renewed my hope of working with my dad. In the spring of 1974, we bought an old 560 Farmall tractor and a four-bottom plow. We did this so we would be more independent. With Dad's help we rented 160 acres from two retiring farmers. With as little family help as possible we were into farming.

The following year we rented an additional 240 acres with an old set of farm buildings including the house we live in today. With a bank loan we purchased a meager line of used farm equipment. We were independent and on our own. As disappointing as it was, there simply was no way to work with my father. I absolutely believe that he wanted for us to work together in the worst way. On the other hand for Jean and me to have any chance of having a healthy, functioning family would require separating from him as much as possible.

> *Here is a lesson: Confront the faults and deficiencies you inherited from your parents so they are not passed on to your children. On the other hand, cultivate the virtues you received from them and pass those on so that your posterity can be blessed for generations. In other words, "Don't throw the baby out with the wash." This is never a good idea because, especially in this instance, it will hurt your babies!*

12

A HOME OF OUR OWN

Jean and I, along with our oldest daughter, Stephanie, moved onto the farm where we presently live on March 1, 1975. It was a rag-tag set of farm buildings that included a beautiful but neglected Victorian-style farmhouse built in 1893 by Elbert T. McGehee.

It is my understanding that the farm was later operated by his son Ralph, who because of the drought and Depression of the 1930s lost the farm to the Farmer's National Bank in Madison. While it was in the bank's possession, the farm was leased to a man with the last name of Doncheski. Later the farm was sold to a Mr. Morritz who was the father of the lady from whom we purchased it in 1987.

I found this old newspaper article concerning Mr. McGehee, which I found rather interesting:

E.T. McGehee of Madison County, Nebraska, has, by dint of general industry, reliable character and straightforward business methods, built up for himself a name and standing second to none in this part of Nebraska. He is still in the maturity of his powers, and commands a host of friends wherever he is known. Mr. McGehee is one of the very oldest settlers in this region, having come here to reside some forty-nine years ago; he now lives in section six, township twenty-one, range one, where he and his family are loved and respected by all. Mr. McGehee is a native of Iowa County, Wisconsin, born April 8, 1850, and is a son of Henderson and Sarah McGehee, both natives of Tennessee.

In 1871 our subjects left his home and came to Madison County, Nebraska, coming by ox team, being four weeks on the way. He took up a homestead in Platte County, Nebraska, nine miles south of Madison City, and after locating on the homestead, built a dugout and lived in this five years; he then built a frame house, hauling the lumber for this house from Columbus, many miles distant. Deer and antelope were plentiful in those days, and occasionally a few elk were to be seen; in 1873, 1874, and 1875, the grasshoppers destroyed all the crops, which made it very hard sailing for the early settler.

In 1893 Mr. McGehee bought the Adair and Martin homestead, his present farm, which he improved, and where he now has a beautiful home. While living on this farm, in 1894, he lost all his crops by the hot winds that prevailed during that season. Mr. McGehee now owns about thirteen hundred and seven acres of fine land, all of which is well improved.

In 1876 Mr. McGehee was united in marriage to Miss Bessie Leach, and Mr. and Mrs. McGehee are the parents of seven children, whose names are as follows: Ralph, Edna, Florence, Ruth, Aria, Mary, and Elberta. They are a prominent family, and, as before stated, are highly respected and esteemed by all who know them, and their friends are many.

Other than the house, the rest of the buildings, which included a granary, horse barn, hog barn, chicken house, ice house and outhouse, were in need of demolition or major renovation. There were weeds growing everywhere. Circling the house yard were huge, ragged stumps, ten to fifteen feet tall, left as spoils of the Dutch-Elm disease.

The house had seen little upkeep in its eighty-year history. The exterior was spotted with bare wood where the paint was peeling. Inside, the plaster was held in place by several layers of wallpaper. Where this had failed, there were hodge-podge patches in the plaster.

In the kitchen all the plaster had come loose, and all four walls and ceiling were patched and painted swimming pool green. There was a tin sink in the corner with a couple small metal cabinets, all of which had changed colors several times, verified by the rust-stained, chipped paint on the corners and wear spots around the handles.

The four walls of this twelve-by-thirteen-foot room had two windows and six doors in Victorian style. There was only one spot for a kitchen range, between the dining room and pantry doors below the soot-lined hole in the chimney, which once held an exhaust pipe that carried the smoke away from a wood-fired cooking stove.

The basement was another story altogether. The soft red brick foundation was crumbling. Numerous bricks in the top row were loose, allowing mice, insects, skunks, and possums to come and go as they pleased. Talk about the wild kingdom.

The grove by the house was populated with numerous Box elder trees. During the summer months these trees were nesting habitats for millions of Box elder bugs. Every fall we were invaded by these pesky creatures. At times these insects were so thick on the basement floor that it was like walking on Rice Krispies. I did my best to stop them, but my efforts were mostly futile.

Upon checking the children one evening as Jean and I returned from a dinner date, I noticed a small unidentified animal dropping in the middle of their playroom floor. Jean and I were mystified by this. I noticed that the cast iron grill covering the air vent had come loose. I bent down and with the use of a flashlight and a mirror discovered a family of baby possums in the cold air return duct. Try as I might, I couldn't get them to come out. It was late and not only was I not in the mood to get them out; I didn't know how. So I just reattached the grill cover to the wall, and we went to bed. Out-of-sight, out-of-mind.

A night or two later we were lying in bed when Jean heard a funny noise. She was certain the sound was coming from the basement, so I got up to check it out. I went down into the basement and heard a noise coming from a large cardboard box in the corner of the room where Jean saved her empty milk jugs for recycling. I opened the box and found three baby possums crawling around in the milk jugs like kids in one of those plastic ball playpens at Chuck E. Cheese.

I captured the critters and figured I had the problem taken care of, but the next night Jean heard another noise when we were lying in bed. I assured her I had taken care of all the little varmints, but I went down anyway to check.

Much to my surprise, two more possums were waiting for me at the foot of the stairs, staring at me as if I was invading their space. So I got rid of these two as well.

The next night, sure enough, we heard more noise from the basement on our way to bed, and I went down again to discover four more little campers. I disposed of those guys, and that was finally the end of our possum intruders.

I later found out they had been residing in the furnace cold air returns. They were able to enter through some missing bricks on the north end of the basement adjacent to a spider-web-strewn dirt floor crawl space. In all, nine possums were living with us.

Those possums weren't our only brush with wildlife.

My feet hit the floor one Sunday morning as the alarm clock went off for church. Within seconds the whole house reeked of a skunk.

Directly under our bedroom was a crawl space, which became a stopping point for animals such as the one that just sprayed or the possums in the previous episode.

Putting my feet on the floor must have startled the smelly varmint. We tried to ignore the smell, but it was virtually impossible.

We went to church anyway. I am sure more than a few people thought a skunk sprayed right outside of church. If you have ever heard the term *sticking like stink to a skunk,* it was proven that day at St. Leonard's. We never divulged our secret to other members of the congregation.

The chronic mouse problem in that old house was yet another issue to be reckoned with. They were on the attack every year from September on. I plugged hole after hole and yet they came. They loved us.

I had a secret place under the kitchen cupboards where I set traps to catch them. I had constructed a plywood barrier to prevent them from entering the kitchen cupboards. On the underside of that barrier I caught the little buggers, one after another.

I checked the traps as regularly as someone else might let their dog out in the morning.

In the evening after the kids were in bed and the house was quiet, we could hear the little critters running across the top side of the cardboard tile ceiling in the family room.

After we purchased the farm, constructing a new basement foundation was the first major remodel project. Since that time we have had no unwanted guests, at least not furry ones. How pleasant this was after battling them for fifteen years. I remember hearing things like, "What a charming old home you have there." I guess the varmints weren't visible from the outside.

Here's the lesson: The body tends to put into play what the mind conceives. Sometime during the year prior to moving into this old house I recall driving past it while hauling a wagon load of grain to the local elevator. As I drove by I said a prayer and thanked God that he might bless us with such a beautiful farm. That was my vision—that this place, which was literally falling down from neglect, was a beautiful farm. At that time it really wasn't beautiful at all. Jean, being much more of a realist, reminded me of that; after all, she put up with a whole bunch more of its deficits than I did. Jean and I worked incessantly for years to make that happen. Today this truly is one of the most beautiful farms in Madison County, Nebraska. With hard work, dreams put into play have a tendency to come true.

13

SHOOTING DOWN A BLACK TUNNEL

Our first child, Stephanie, was born in 1974, the same year I began farming on my own. I loved being married, and I loved being a dad. I doubt I was aware of it at the time, but I'm sure one of the reasons I got into farming was to seek the affirmation of my father. The frustration over this along with the financial downturn in the farming sector resulted in unfiltered anger. I was angry at my father. I was angry at Jean. I was angry at the world.

I felt I had failed my family and especially my father. Nothing I ever did seemed to please him and I couldn't find it in my heart to accept this injustice.

I became an abusive person to live with. I share many personality traits with my father and was well on track to ending up just like him—abusive and controlling.

The boiling point came when I began questioning my faith. I left the church and went to the local Lutheran church for a brief period. I went to a Baptist church too, looking for answers.

In the summertime when I was out spraying corn in the fields, I'd listen to Christian radio. I listened to preachers who claimed they had all the answers, and preached a feel-good doctrine with sugar-coated messages like, "You'll have no problems at all as long as you have faith in God. And by the way, please send the check."

The "send the check" part is facetious. After a while, I had difficulty buying into a feel-good faith that ignored the real-life problems I was facing every day. After all, what did feeling good have to do with paying off my debt? Did feeling good take care of our family?

I was searching for answers, hoping to find an easy way out of my predicament, but I didn't find it there.

Through faith and prayers God has an interesting way of working things out. I credit the love of God and his divine intervention for bringing me in contact with two very special individuals.

Dr. Dick Sanders was a psychologist whom Jean and I visited numerous times dealing with the effects of my dysfunctional upbringing that included some serious questions concerning my Catholic faith. I respected him as a sound thinker. Whether or not he was that great of a psychologist, I'll never be sure, but he became a good friend to me personally. His daughter Sally was one of the musicians who sang at our wedding, which is how I met him in the first place.

I was visiting with Dr. Sanders one day, contemplating my spiritual crisis, when he made a profound statement. I asked him whether I should return to the Catholic Church or look for something else to fulfill my emptiness. His answer, although indirect, was incredibly tactful. "Leon," he said, "the Catholic faith is a very sound theology."

There it was; one sentence. No more, no less. One sentence in the middle of a storm coming from a person I respected. My life was upside down and I was grab-bagging for anything solvent that would make things better, but there are no quick fixes in life. Problems are either handled or mishandled, but quick fixes always come back to bite you.

This one sentence from a highly intelligent man sent up a red flag that simplified things for me. The Catholic faith *was* a sound theology, and a theology I had learned growing up.

As a little kid, I learned all about my Catholic faith, but it wasn't until I hit rock bottom in my faith development that I came to accept the reality of what I had learned as a child.

I was, up until this point, an angry person who lived only to gain the acceptance of his father. I had nearly forgotten who "I" was as a person because I was so consumed by trying to please Gilbert Weiland.

Even after I had failed at farming, during those first few years in the door business I longed so much for his acceptance. Every time I heard a car come up the driveway I'd stand up and look out the window of my barn office to see if it was my dad coming to see me. I was looking for acknowledgment from him. Hell, anything would have been enough, just something to let me know he cared. And now I was willing to throw away the entire foundation of my faith just because I was angry?

Dr. Sanders made me realize how much I needed my faith.

Jean was a rock too. She never budged. As close as I may have come to abandoning Catholicism altogether, the thought never occurred to her once. She was Catholic and she wasn't leaving. Her foundation was already set, but, like our old farmhouse, my foundation still needed some work. A few wise people pointed this out to me too, hoping I'd realize that a life of faith is something that can and *should* be experienced together with your spouse.

Many nights as a young married man, after Jean and the kids had gone to bed, I'd go out for long walks by myself in the comfort of the moonlit sky. Nebraska is known for its sunsets, but a late night walk guided by the light of the moon is a spectacle to behold.

My life was a disaster. Yet somehow in the storm of the wolves biting me in the butt for money I didn't have, and promises I couldn't deliver, a life filled with anger and regret over past failures and the empty feeling that I was all alone, I found peace. In a world where I had no advocate and no champion, I could go out on those long walks at night and find peace. I could feel the eternal presence of God in my life.

The peace I found was not in worrying about mistakes I'd made in the past, nor was it in anticipating what was waiting for me in the future, because the future looked so bleak. The peace was only in the present and somehow knowing that God was real. For that gift I am so thankful.

By 1981 we had spent the previous seven years farming in my hometown of Madison, Nebraska. Things went well at first. We made some money farming during that time and figured I had a fairly good idea of what was required to be successful.

During that seven-year period farmland prices tripled. Twice during that period I had saved enough money for a down payment on an 80-acre farm, only to see farmland appreciate in value beyond what I had saved. I had put away nearly $30,000, yet hadn't gained any ground whatsoever on owning my dream.

Finally, by 1979, five years after we started farming, we had saved enough for a down payment to purchase a farm for roughly $1,000 an acre. It was a 108-acre farm that ran along Taylor Creek. Taylor Creek was a narrow, deep spring-fed stream that extended from Madison northwest for about eight miles. The abundance of water in the stream supplied water for irrigation. The farm had some rough spots where it had been neglected. We developed the farm, removing trees and installing irrigation to make the land more suitable for growing crops. We borrowed all the money needed to make these improvements.

The value of farmland was appreciating at a breakneck rate, so in 1980 we purchased an additional farm and another in 1981, all with 100 percent financing. Using debt as a hedge against inflation was the rule of the day. I had a hunch that land appreciation would make us rich over the long haul. While the idea may have been good in theory, and even in practice twenty or thirty years earlier, the economy didn't cooperate with this strategy in the late 1970s and early 1980s.

This strategy would have worked fine during any five-year period from 1960 on, except for the five-year period in which I tried it. Looking back on that land purchase spree today, I realize that I simply hadn't lived enough history to recognize the financial scourge awaiting me. I thought I'd be able to leverage my assets to get ahead, but the high interest rates and depreciation of real estate changed the rules of the game when I was already in over my head.

I have a friend, several years younger than I, who began buying farmland in about 1990. He has done extremely well. The climate in the farm sector has been favorable for him and his family as well. There have been no big downturns in the farm economy since it fell apart in the 1980s.

We simply were born at the wrong time. My father went into a great deal of debt in the late 1960s to expand our farm with a modern, automated cattle feeding unit. It was equipped with three seventy- to eighty-feet tall, glass lined feed storage units. The cattle feed was unloaded out of the bottom of these structures with a drive chain equipped with hooks that tore through the solid packed forage that had been compacted with tons and tons of forage blown in at the top from the alfalfa and corn crops we harvested throughout the summer and fall.

The silage, as it is called, was delivered along the top of the feed trough via a twenty-four-inch-wide rubber belt while a rotary brush moved up and down the length of the belt, pushing the cattle feed into a trough where the cattle consumed it at their leisure. It was a marvelous way of feeding the animals.

This device, along with the many extra cattle it would feed, cost a rather large sum of money—money that my dad did not have. However, he was born a generation earlier. Had he done the same thing at the same time as me, he more than likely would have had the same financial disaster.

Needless to say numerous farmers from his generation were caught up in the land buying frenzy of the late 1970s. I'm not sure where these farmers acquired such a bold attitude. Perhaps they were unsatisfied with lengthy careers that had yet to yield the kind of financial success they anticipated, or maybe they were simply partnering with a son who was following his own dream. I do know that, for those older farmers, experiencing this downturn was devastating. More than a few suicides were committed during that time by members of my dad's generation.

By the fall of 1983, we sold one farm and quit-claim deeded the other two back to their original owners. In that same year I drafted a financial statement. It was apparent we owed the bank way more than we were worth. We had invested boatloads of borrowed money in farms and equipment. One expense followed another. We could not keep up with paying the 15 to 18 percent interest.

The debt snowballed with unpaid interest added to loan principal. It was like getting run over in a financial stampede.

We had four young children at home and a fifth on the way. We were definitely in major financial trouble.

Here is the lesson: Pain, whatever kind, is a potent educator. Whether it is yours or someone else's, be a student of it. Don't ever forget it. Instead let it hone you, inspire you, toughen you, but don't let it break you. Let it make you more compassionate, but not soften your resolve for change because the change it causes will prod you to a height you never would have accomplished in its absence.

14

HOW GOD OPENED WEILAND DOORS

Winters in Nebraska can drag on, especially if you're a grain farmer. They're long, dead periods of waiting and hoping—waiting for the temperatures to warm and hoping the weather cooperates to make your crop year a profitable one.

For Jean and me, the winter of 1983 was an especially long one full of more uncertainty than we'd ever encountered. The extremely negative balance sheet I had compiled in November showed our farm business more than $100,000 in the red. I simply had to find another way to earn additional income.

I had gone to Jim Housel a few years previous looking for part-time work. Because I didn't raise livestock in the winter, as many farmers did, I had time for winter employment. Jim, with the help of his wife, Tillie, manufactured fiberglass pontoon boats. I figured he might need another handyman around to help with the work.

"Yeah, I'll hire you," he said to my request, in his typical, matter-of-fact tone.

I couldn't believe it.

Jim and Tillie lived in a remodeled Massey Ferguson implement dealership a half mile north of Madison. Walking through the front glass door would either take you into their kitchen to the right or into the shop to the left. He didn't have to go to work; work was always right there. If he ever got stumped with a mechanical problem, he'd go into the residential part of the building, have a bite to eat, and think about his problem.

He loved nachos with cheese, sandwiches, and french fries—all the good stuff.

Jim was smart, very smart, and industrious. He was a self-taught craftsman with a passion for tinkering.

Not only did he hire me, Jim was more than fair in what he paid me. Eight dollars per hour was a lot to shell out for part-time help during the winter, especially to a kid who didn't know anything. So I began helping him make pontoon boats.

The bodies of these pontoon boats were made almost entirely of molded fiberglass. While a few of the parts were outsourced, most of the major components were fabricated in his shop.

Jim was about fifteen years older than I. I learned a lot from him such as how to spray fiberglass, how to create mechanical drawings of parts, and, most importantly, how to construct something out of nothing—or at least very little.

Our tools were primitive and limited, especially considering we were making boats, a normally glamorous profession.

Jim had such a fascinating mechanical mind. He could look at just about anything and instantly dissect its working parts. It seemed, to me at least, there wasn't a problem he couldn't solve. I've seen few people before or since who had the mechanical talents of Jim Housel.

Tillie told me I, like Jim, had a knack for mechanical things. I took that as a huge compliment because I truly admired his ability.

So when I went to Jim in November 1983 with my idea of making furniture to sell at craft shows, he replied with the most profound statement anyone ever said to me, "Gus, I don't think that'll work."

Gus was a nickname my Grandpa Weiland gave me. I cannot remember not having that name, so I must have been rather young. The name caught on and by the time I reached grade school I was commonly referred to as Gus. Today I am commonly referred to as Leon, so when someone addresses me with the name Gus, I know this person has known me for a long time.

However shocking it may have been, I had to own up to the cold reality that cobbling around homemade furniture wasn't the solution to my financial predicament. Jim was a friend and confidant, so when he told me something, he didn't mince words.

Jim did share another idea with me that winter, however. It was advice that would change my life forever. He had fabricated some fiberglass door panels for the pork processing plant in Madison. He thought if I could find ten other packing plants that would buy them, I might be able to make enough money to cover my family's living expenses, continue farming, and possibly even cut into my extensive debt.

My home town of Madison was home to a pork processing plant called Madison Foods. It had been built by a group of investors. As the plant grew and evolved, like so many others around the country, it was eventually acquired by a company called Iowa Beef Processors, Incorporated.

IBP was one of the country's largest beef packers and pork processors. The company was later acquired by Tyson Foods in 2001.

So there I was, a small fish diving into a big sea. I had no knowledge of any kind about the door business. I had no knowledge about doing business with world-class companies. I guess you could say that my ignorance didn't convince me that I couldn't do it, so I did.

At the time, the thought of selling doors to the largest red meat processor in the world was a pipe dream to be sure; but a pipe dream is a dream, and it was mine. I was like the bumble bee that didn't realize all the data should have proved that flying was impossible. And so I began with some basic tools gleaned from my farm shop, an idea sprinkled with hope and my eye on a dream.

In December of that year our youngest child and only son, Carl, was born. The pregnancy was incredibly difficult for Jean. During the delivery she hemorrhaged profusely, requiring seven pints of blood and an additional eight pints the following week, along with an emergency surgery to stop the bleeding.

Even after her release from the hospital, she felt rundown and exhausted—more than she had during any of her previous four deliveries. Days turned to weeks and still her health didn't improve. We went to doctor after doctor looking for answers. We saw doctors in nearby Norfolk and doctors in Omaha, but nobody could explain her mysterious illness.

She felt cold and lethargic, like a woman twice her age. One particular doctor diagnosed her with a severe case of arthritis. She was told she'd just have to adjust her lifestyle to allow for the pain and severe energy loss. We didn't buy that one bit.

As you may imagine, this left our situation looking pretty bleak. We were up to our ears in debt with Jean being very ill and five needy youngsters at home. All I could think about was how desperate our situation was and how bleak the future looked.

One cold February morning while Jean and the kids were still in bed, I was sitting in the kitchen, thinking and praying. It's a practice I'd gotten into regularly, and still maintain to this day. I prayed for help. I prayed for health. I prayed for anything that could be a solution to our problems.

As I was sitting there filled with worry and regret about the path my life had taken, I heard a voice say, "Leon, I'm going to bless you with blessings you've never even dreamed of."

One sentence. That was all. No more, no less. All I could do was look around the room, trying to explain this phenomenon. But it was silent.

Jean was sick. We were broke. The Department of Social Services had turned down our requests for financial aid because I owned an old snowmobile, which they viewed as a nonessential asset. At the bottom of my life, in the lowest of lows, I couldn't even get food stamps.

When I was told that a $300 John Deere snowmobile was the only thing left to my name, I knew we were in trouble.

Going broke is like shooting down a black tunnel at lightning speed with no way of knowing what's waiting for you at the other end. And its ramifications are even bleaker for a married man with five children under the age of nine. This voice calling out to me was the most bizarre thing imaginable. It spoke to me, directly to me.

I was the head of a family I couldn't support, seemingly caught in a hopeless situation. Supposedly being blessed beyond anything I'd ever dreamed? I was an owner of nothing, except an idea given to me by a friend for building doors.

One day in January 1984, I went out to an old shed on the farm where we lived and put that idea to work.

When we had moved onto the farm, the sides of this building were leaning out causing the roof peak to sag about a foot. The dirt floor was high in the middle from eighty years of dried dirt deposited there by farm machinery pulled through the brown Nebraska mud. The south end of the building was completely open as the doors had been ripped off in some remote wind storm.

Sometime in the late seventies our landlord paid for the materials, which allowed me to level out and pour a concrete floor and straighten up the sides and roof. The exterior of this twenty-by-forty-foot shed was covered with barn siding, littered with cracks and crevices that let in the cold January air. The temperature was almost unbearable inside.

If I was going to work in that old shed, I at least had to be able to feel my own hands, so the first thing I did was fabricate two door panels from two old large sliding doors my cousin Bob Jurgens had removed from his snowmobile dealership storage building. Along with the doors he also gave me the track and hardware required to install them on my shed. Because they were much too large, I was required to cut them down to a smaller size, which left me with half a door panel I did not need.

In addition to installing doors that covered the south end of the building, I plugged all the holes in the exterior siding with auto body bondo. Installing the doors and covering the holes may have kept cold air from coming in, but it still didn't supply any heat. I had to find a way to make the working conditions inside the shed tolerable.

My solution was to construct a heating stove from a discarded 300-gallon cylindrical fuel barrel. I torched a hole in one side of the barrel and welded on a hinged door assembly I had fabricated from some pieces of scrap iron to cover the hole. So I could stand this fire box upright I welded four legs on one end.

After getting the barrel balanced on its legs, I cut holes through the roof of the shed and the top of the barrel. I fashioned a flue out of salvaged eight-inch auger tubing. I salvaged an old electric exhaust barn fan and attached it to the barrel with a bracket, aiming it so it would blow air directly toward the outside of the barrel.

Fuel for this stove was gleaned from dead trees I found along the creek bordering the east side of the farm. This apparatus worked extremely well. At times the stove heated the shop so effectively that I had to crack the windows to cool the shop to comfortably work in there.

Because my intention was to build doors I still didn't have a work bench large enough to support the product. To solve this problem I stretched the leftover half door panel over six 55-gallon salvaged resin drums. This workbench was a mainstay in our door business for several years. This makeshift shop along with a small Sears radial arm saw, a hand drill, a hammer, and nails were the tools I had to get into the door business.

Here is the lesson: Weiland Doors was dug out of the ground with little more than a rock, a club, hope, and dreams. Failure was never an option. If you want to succeed, put your head down and bear into it. Make no excuse for yourself and get to work. Eat, drink, and breathe your goal. Pray constantly. You will accomplish what your mind sets in motion. The more tenacious your actions become, the more difficult it will be to stop you. I doubt God opens many doors for people who aren't pushing on the door and crying for help.

15

THE EARLY YEARS

The first product I constructed when I was getting started, even before building any real doors, was a miniature model door to show potential buyers. It was a tiny IBP green door, twelve inches wide and twenty-eight inches tall, with a little window in it. I also produced some color brochures, but this miniature model was my primary visual aid.

Looking back, it's amazing I was able to sell anything at all. I must have been a convincing salesman.

When it actually came time to build the real doors, my years spent under Jim's wing came in handy. While many of my doors were uniform, others had to be tailored precisely to fit the specifications of the buyer. Some of the first electric-power-operated doors that I made required many special parts. I remember spending months laboring over drawings for parts that made up only a fraction of the entire door assembly, yet were essential to its operation.

Our first door panels were constructed with two three-quarter-inch-thick sheets of plywood fastened together back to back and subsequently sprayed with polyester resin mixed with chopped fiberglass strand. After drying, the surfaces and corners were sanded, smoothed, and top-coated with white polyester paint material. They were crude and archaic looking to say the least. But they were sturdy. The doors were extremely heavy.

Later I found that my customers wanted their doors to be somewhat lighter yet still the same thickness as a standard door, so I had to make adjustments in my design.

Before this time the meat packing industry used primarily steel doors. There was little competition for my early fiberglass doors primarily because typical fiberglass doors at that time were expensive and also because the federal meat inspectors did not have certain requirements. However, at that time most of the plants used salt on the floors for food safety. This alone limited the durability of steel doors.

In certain plant areas steel doors would rust through in six months or less. We provided the solution. Our fiberglass doors, even though they were not as pretty as the competition's, were extremely durable and, in addition, did not rust out. For less than $200 we provided them with a walk-through door that would last for years. It wasn't long before Weiland Fiberglass Doors were used in virtually every major meat plant in the central U.S.

That first year, door sales totaled $14,000. I was able to pocket about half that amount. It was helpful, but not enough.

My second year in business I discovered there was a need in meat packing plants for stainless steel personnel lockers. I contracted with a company in Norfolk about making the parts for the lockers. They agreed to fabricate the parts for me because I didn't have any machinery to shear and bend the parts.

I built a rather odd-looking spring-assisted clamping jig to hold the stainless steel parts in place for welding. My mother always told me that necessity is the motherhood of invention. That was never better displayed than here.

I was hungry for success and had a passion for building. I read an article once about the term *flow* as it pertains to working in the area of your talents. Can you imagine Magic Johnson doing anything other than playing basketball, Warren Buffett doing anything other than investing, or Louie Armstrong doing anything other than playing the trumpet? I had found my flow. I could feel it. It was fantastic!

That second year sales amounted to over $60,000.

That same year I bought a slightly used Ford F250 three-quarter ton flatbed diesel pickup. Later I constructed a display of several types of working doors that mounted on the truck's bed. It was a rather extensive brochure to say the least. However it demonstrated that I at least could do what I said I could do: build doors.

I was a little guy from a little town who mostly didn't have a clue what he was doing. This display and the miniature

Me and my door display

model got me through the doors and onto the spec sheets of the largest meat packing firms in the world.

When I was out selling doors, I'd offer all my customers a free door to try. Even today I'll tell customers to try a door and if they don't like it, I'll send a truck to pick it up at no cost whatsoever. That practice helped me get a lot of business. Even though, in all, I gave away fewer than five doors, the promise that I would put my product on the line was impressive enough to cause my customers to be curious about why I was so sure of my product.

> *Here is a lesson: I have always pondered a bible verse that simply states that blessing will be returned to us in the same measure that we bless others. Most likely that verse is referring to the joy that awaits us in heaven. However it seems to me a life of sharing the blessings which have been bestowed on us is rewarded long before we reach our eternal goal. In no way am I suggesting God can be manipulated or that giving is some sort of religious investment, because it might very well be that a generous heart is the only gift God wants you to have.*

Putting myself in my customer's shoes, I can only imagine what they thought when they saw me pull up in this flatbed diesel pickup with a miniature model door display strapped on the back. I probably looked like a traveling salesman from the Sunday cartoons. Maybe they just assumed anyone who put so much time and effort into his truck display (as a hands-on brochure) couldn't possibly have anything other than honest intentions.

Those initial days of selling doors made for early mornings, late nights, and a lot of chaos in between. We were in a precarious situation caring for young children while starting a shot-in-the-dark business with no money to fall back on.

Jean's health failed to improve, so in May of that year, just five months after Carl was born and the advent of Weiland Doors, we traveled to the Mayo Clinic in Rochester, Minnesota. After a battery of tests, the doctors there finally gave us an answer that we hadn't heard yet.

Jean was diagnosed with Sheehan's syndrome. The excessive hemorrhaging during childbirth led to prolonged periods of extremely low blood pressure, causing a lot of damage to her body, including her pituitary gland. The doctors told us that if Jean had gone another six months without treating the disease, she would have died. Sheehan's syndrome was affecting her thyroid functions, her adrenal functions, and her gonadal functions.

The doctors prescribed prednisone and some other drugs to combat these problems. They weren't the "cure-all" remedy we had hoped for, but the drugs stabilized her condition. She still had low immunity to diseases and was continuously fatigued, but at last we had a name to put on the face of her strange ailment.

We hired an employee during our second year of business to keep up with the demands we were getting for doors and lockers. Shortly after, we moved our operation from that shed to an old barn on our farm. This was my first corporate office.

At one time, that barn housed three hundred or so head of hogs and it smelled like it. No matter how many times we cleaned, we couldn't completely get rid of that hog smell.

The barn had a hay loft, which we removed and renovated so the ceiling was twelve feet high. We insulated the barn and sectioned it off, one side as a parts room and the other for my office.

I didn't have a computer in my office; it wouldn't have survived those cold winter months when we turned the heat off at night. My most lavish office supply was an old red dial-up desk phone. I heated the office with an outdated propane catalytic heater.

By 1986, our third year in business, we grossed $120,000 in sales of doors and stainless steel lockers. The price of stainless steel had risen to the point at which it was not cost-effective for use as material for building personnel lockers.

We doubled my sales again the next year, and it wasn't long before we had annual sales of over half a million dollars.

Farming didn't seem to fit into our future plans, so we decided to sell all the farm equipment.

The bank where we had accumulated so much debt approached me about a settlement. Together, we arranged a payment plan that would allow me to pay off my debt without my interest compounding. Six years later our debt was gone. A year after that we paid a lump sum to cover the remaining interest and deducted the amount on our tax return.

Since we leased the farm where we lived and started our business, it was never in jeopardy. Because of the 1980s farm crisis, this farm too had lost a great deal of its value. So when it came up for sale in 1987, we were also able to buy the farm for a rock bottom price. Today it has appreciated immensely from the purchase price. By that time we were doing better financially than we ever had farming—ever.

The truth is, farming wasn't working out and certainly wasn't factoring into our future. But throughout those failed attempts at farming and working with Jim Housel, I hadn't failed to learn. In addition to his intimate mechanical knowledge, Jim knew how to sell. His example demonstrated to me over and over again the value of making that emotional connection with a potential buyer and the importance of treating people with caring and respect no matter who they were.

People in the market for a particular service or product prefer to do business with people they like. It's not always about selling a product, but selling yourself and your customer service. It's probably safe to say that if it wasn't for Jim, we wouldn't be where we are today—the whole idea for making doors, after all, was his.

Seven years after I got into the door business, Jim suddenly died of a heart attack brought on by a case of pneumonia. I was devastated. While he was alive, Jim was my cheerleader. He had done so much for me and my family. We shared a love of building things along with a passion for bullshit. Building and bullshit; I have never known anyone who did it better than Jim. I don't know of anyone who loves it more than I do. Losing him left a hole in my life unlike any I have ever known.

Jim always seemed afraid of pricing his boats above what the average family could afford. He wanted to be sure that his boats were affordable to as many people as possible. Therefore, he probably did not charge as much as he could have. I suspected that many times he paid his employees as much or more than he paid himself because they had young families to support. I think this kindness may have made it rather difficult for Tillie when he died.

Because so much of his boat manufacturing business relied on his special talents, it limited the potential buyers for the business. Tillie was left with a business that wasn't worth as much as it could have been.

On the other hand, if a man's true wealth is determined by what he has that cannot be sold, he was truly a rich person. My estimation of him alone was priceless.

Sometimes I reflect on that promise that was made to me years ago on that cold winter morning in my kitchen. I've pondered it often. Was it merely my imagination playing tricks on me? Or was there an angel looking out for my family and me? Maybe it was both.

One thing is certain, it was a promise that's been fulfilled and continues to be fulfilled today. Everything that's happened to my family and me since that day, including the opportunity to sit down and write my thoughts for others to see, is a blessing beyond what I would ever have dreamed during those dire times.

Those dark days of being broke and hopeless remind me of summers spent as a kid in the cornfields of Nebraska. My siblings and I used to walk through our cornfields looking for cockleburs. Cockleburs are weeds that if left to grow unchecked take over cornfields in waves so thick they'll choke out an entire crop of corn. They're weeds that absolutely have to be controlled if you want to produce a good crop. Farmers who didn't control the cocklebur population in their fields didn't fare too well at harvest time.

We'd walk through cornfields with a corn knife that resembled a machete, whacking out all the cocklebur weeds as we went. We would usually work in teams of two or three people. Walking through those fields in the stifling summer heat was like walking through a furnace wearing a rubber suit; the air was suffocating. In the afternoons the summer heat was overpowering.

There was pollen in the air and the sharp edges of the corn leaves would chafe our arms as we walked. Walking through endless rows of eight-feet-tall corn was a lesson in perseverance.

As a youngster, the corn was usually much taller than I was, and I couldn't see more than five feet in any one direction. I could only follow the path of the corn rows. It was hard work and the only way to get through it was to keep walking. If I stopped, the only thing gained was more time in this stifling environment. I just had to keep moving.

But there were times when I'd come to the top of a hill where the soil was eroded causing the corn to be much shorter. There I'd catch a glimpse of the world. I could breathe the fresh air and see for miles. Those brief moments were my relief from the solemn monotony of walking for cockleburs as we commonly called it. It's a metaphor for life.

Just like cockleburs, there are things in our lives that, if not taken care of, will overpower us. There are times in life when it seems as if we're walking and walking and the corn is just getting taller and taller. The heat is suffocating and unrelenting. It's seems as if there's no way out. Life can be tough unless you're taller than the corn. The only choice is to keep going.

And of course there are times when, like in the cornfield, we reach the top of the hill in the corn and we can see farther than the bleak circumstances surrounding us. The birth of our door company was one of those times. My beautiful wife, Jean, was so ill sometimes she could barely walk. There were bills we couldn't pay. We had five young children who needed constant care. We lost three farms due to financial setbacks.

And somehow in the middle of all this turmoil God opened Weiland Doors and continues to do so every day. His promise to me that cold, bleak morning has been kept. The blessings continue to be added in remarkable ways every day.

Here is the lesson: There will be times when it will take all your energy just to put one foot in front of the other. If that is all you have, then do that. Every step, no matter how labored, will take you one step away from where you are. Keep moving.

16

A DREAMER'S DREAM TEAM

Several years ago I attended a retirement party for a gentleman who was a job superintendent for a longtime customer of Weiland Doors. This fellow was popular with the people who worked under him. Along with his crew, he built processing facilities for some of the largest food companies in the United States.

The crowd that night included everyone in the company who could come, along with numerous customers and vendors. There was an aura there that couldn't be ignored. Throughout the evening, person after person stood up to tell the crowd about how great the company was and how fulfilling a work environment my friend had created for his employees over the years.

All the people who spoke couldn't stop raving about how much they valued their jobs and the friendships they'd formed at the company. Vendors and customers alike all remarked at how much they cared for each other during the years they had shared together in business.

This outpouring of camaraderie was both heartfelt and inspiring. I wasn't surprised. For years my experience with them was equally as satisfying. They were simply a great bunch of folks with whom to do business. However, until that night I had been unable to put my finger on what made them a remarkable company.

Late in the evening, after a flurry of testimonials, the emcee did a last call for anyone else having thoughts to share with the crowd. I just couldn't resist.

I got the microphone in my hands, stood up and explained to the crowd who I was and why I was there that night. I told them how I always admired their company and it wasn't until this night that I figured out why.

From the company president on down, these folks just flat out loved each other. Respect was the rule. This included their employees, their customers, and their vendors. We were all considered part of their team. We were all made to feel like integral players in the company's success. They had created a family atmosphere unlike any I had ever seen before in the business world, and I was sure to let everyone there know that I felt privileged to be part of the group that night.

The truth is I didn't just feel included on that night alone, I felt included every day from the first time I'd done business with them.

That night it was proven to me that business could be extremely successful if carried on in that fashion. I was inspired to work even more diligently to see that my company, Weiland Doors, operated in the same way. It's that same atmosphere I try to create with everyone in my life. The makeup of Weiland Doors revolves around the idea of family. My entire life is family centered. Why should my business be any different?

During my first year in business I worked exclusively on my own. Weiland Doors was a one-man operation. Me. I set up my shop, built the doors, and sold them all by myself.

Jean was really sick, and with the young kids at home, I made sure I was never out of town selling doors more than two days a week. And I always made sure that I never traveled so far that I couldn't make the return trip that night.

One of my trips during my second year of business took me to Dubuque Packing Company in Le Mars, Iowa. The maintenance superintendent there was a crusty old fellow who used expletives as terms of endearment. For some reason he liked me, and I liked him. He rather reminded me of my Grandpa Weiland. I was familiar with his kind of personality. While many were probably offended by him, I was not. I simply delved through his crust into that big heart he seemed to shield like some sort of treasure.

Bill Grady was one of those guys who gave me a chance. As we were walking through his plant, he asked me if I could make some vertical slide doors for his north dock. I responded that I was sure I could. Now I had seen doors like this, but I had never made one. So I went to work. I came up with a design and four weeks later Bill had three new doors. The design was somewhat awkward, but it worked with some minor changes. Bill seemed to ignore the deficiencies. He said the doors worked just fine. I was probably my own biggest critic.

Here is the lesson: Customers will overlook your sins if they like you. When I first started in the door business, I knew very little. No surprise to

*anyone, yet over and over my customers gave me
the opportunity to serve them. I was honest, sincere,
and hard working. I believe that is the reason I
succeeded against all the odds. People just flat like
to have people like that on their team.*

That same year Mr. Grady asked if I thought I could
make him some stainless steel personnel lockers. Since
this item would require a different set of skills and tools,
I contacted Arkfeld Manufacturing Company. They gave
me some advice on how to construct sets of stainless steel
lockers. I did the design work myself and went back to Bill
with an estimate.

Bill approved an order for thirty-two of these lockers,
so I contracted with Arkfeld to construct the parts. While
they made the parts, I fabricated a welding jig. This jig was
a frame with a series of spring-loaded hold-downs that
kept all the parts in place while they were permanently
welded together.

As I look back on this I must say it was quite an ingenious
contraption. I used this method to fabricate thirty-two
stainless steel personnel lockers and several hundred the
following year.

The locker business was a short-term venture. The price
of stainless steel increased by about 50 percent, which made
the lockers cost more than the plants were willing to pay.

That was another turning point. With that I decided to
concentrate my efforts on the door side of our business.

It became clear that I couldn't handle the workload
myself, so I decided to hire an employee. By my third year in

business, I hired another employee and concentrated solely on the managerial aspects of my business: growing the company, selling more doors, and cultivating relationships with customers.

One quality you're sure to find if you wander the shop of Weiland Doors is a mutual respect between me and my employees. I have always been well aware that growing our company wouldn't be possible without their contributions. They know that although I'm chiefly responsible for managing the company now, there was a time I've done the exact same job as theirs. When they know the head of the company has done the same work they're doing, it's a direct indication that their work is valuable to our success.

IBP, headquartered in Dakota City, Nebraska, was our first and biggest customer. Many of the men who graced the offices there were little guys at one time who put their hearts on the line and went to work. Many of them began their tenure working on the production line doing jobs like stripping guts and boning heads. This company wasn't managed by a group of softies. They were a tough bunch to say the least, and they weren't interested in glitz; they wanted durability. And durability is what I had to offer. They quite literally walked through the blood to get to where they were. I walked right along with them.

During my first year in business, I was called on by one of their maintenance superintendents to repair a large hole that had been punctured in the side of a very large fiberglass blood tank. The tank was outside in 20-degree weather. The hole, even though it was only about three feet from the bottom, was in a place that made it impossible to repair from the outside. There was an eighteen-inch-diameter access about four feet off the floor that allowed me to get inside with my tools.

As I slid into the tank I discovered about ten inches of semifrozen animal blood creeping up around my ankles. I soon knew why they most likely called me. Nonetheless, I repaired the hole and sent them the bill.

Here is the lesson: If you want to make a lot of money, do the jobs no one else wants to do, the jobs no one else knows how to do, and the jobs that no one else has the guts to do. If the job is easy, anyone can do it and it probably won't pay enough to take your family out for a dinner of Big Macs and fries.

The people who build our doors are skilled with their hands. They may not have college diplomas hanging on their walls at home, but they have an eye for building things, whether it's furniture, mechanical, or electrical. My boys are talented fabricators. If I draw them a picture of what to build, they can go out and do it.

With varying talents, starting with administrative personnel right on over to the fiberglass technicians, they work together to see the big picture and finish projects correctly and on time.

The team we've assembled at Weiland Doors is a team that appreciates the values of teamwork and spirituality. Not all my employees belong to the same church, but they all respect each other's right to lead spiritual lives of their own.

When I'm looking to hire an employee, I look for family people first. You could probably say I'm picky in that regard. I've found that family people typically understand the concept of teamwork and like to belong to some sort of family environment in the workplace. When one of us needs to go somewhere to do something during the workday, whether it be to a daughter's dentist appointment or a son's basketball game, everybody else understands and picks up the slack so they're able to do that.

Family-oriented people need an employer who understands the value of what goes on outside of work. Many mornings at work, the first thing I do is walk through the shop and talk to everyone to see how they're doing. I'll ask them how their weekend went or how their kids are doing in school. This lets them know that I care, but it also builds friendships that last for years.

Over the years I have noticed employers who use up their employees like machinery, similar to a "when it's worn out discard it and get a new one mentality." Along with "we will use you every day until there is little left of you, after which you can go home to your family." It has always been my goal to be sure this doesn't happen at Weiland Doors.

I think it is so important for our employees to have a vibrant family life, which is impossible with the employer attitudes I just described. Associating with such a great group of people has done wonders for my company's success. Who knows where Weiland Doors would be if not for the commitment of the team we've assembled. It's because of these people that Weiland Doors continues to be a presence in our industry.

Our doors are listed on the spec sheets of major players in the food industry such as ConAgra, Tyson, and Hormel. My hope is that by maintaining the cohesiveness of a small, close-knit group of people who work in a dignified manner, our company will continue to be successful. I never want my business to negatively affect the home lives of our people.

We've instituted an incentive program that rewards them with more pay for greater productivity, but if my employees want time off for their families, they can have it. If anyone comes through our doors and doesn't want to be part of this team, my employees see to it that I understand the need for that person to go elsewhere for employment. We work for each other, not against each other.

I was visiting a customer a few years ago, talking business at first, but quickly the conversation turned to our personal lives. We talked a lot about our business attitudes and the similarities in our life stories. This man was obviously very successful in his company. He worked out of a gigantic corner office with windows on two sides overlooking a small lake and gardens.

"How about your kids? How are they doing?" I asked.

"Well," he said, "my kids didn't turn out so well."

He quickly changed the subject. I didn't press him. There became a painful look in his eye at the mention of his children. Who knows what happened? I didn't know and I didn't want to open up a wound, so our meeting soon ended and we both went our separate ways. As I was leaving his office, I couldn't get over the fact that this man had done so well at his job, yet his kids, so he claimed, "didn't turn out so well."

What a disappointment. Who knows what really happened? The man had labored tirelessly to provide for his family, but in the end, something was still missing—something that his family most likely really needed.

I'm so blessed that when I leave work at the end of the day, Jean is there when I go home. Jean and I have five beautiful children. Anyone who knows me will find that rarely can I go five minutes into a conversation without bringing up at least one of them. Jean has been my cheerleader from the start. Even through all the difficult times she has been there bonding our home team, sharing the ups and downs, and helping me keep balance in my life. She is the heart and soul of the Weiland family.

17

THE MILLION-DOLLAR WHORE

A young man walked into a massive high-rise office building one day. He approached the reception desk in the building's lobby. A beautiful young lady with long beautiful hair, glistening eyes and a smile that brightened the room, looked up from her work and asked, "What can I do for you today?"

"I'm here to see your purchasing people," he replied hesitantly. He was clearly taken aback by her beauty.

"May I help you?" she again asked.

"I'm sure you can, but first I need to ask you a question." He stumbled a bit, then asked, "Would you sleep with me for a million dollars?"

She hesitated at first, but after a moment or two thought, "A million dollars is a lot of money. Yeah, I think I will."

"Really?" he said. "A million bucks is a lot of money, how about a half million?" She came back with the same reply.

And so it went, he making the offer and she answering in the affirmative until they got down to $50. At that she exclaimed, "What do you think I am, a whore or something?"

He simply stated, "Young lady, that fact was established at the million-dollar offer. We now are only negotiating the price."

My brother Vern told me this story several years ago. I have always thought that it was meaningful in that it has been my experience that there are those who believe integrity comes in varying degrees—that shoplifting or lying to your insurance company about a claim is different than robbing a bank. And if that's so, it can be sold in varying degrees as well. I have a difficult time with that.

I once had a call from a guy in Chicago who wanted to buy a group of doors from me. I quoted the price to him with COD (Cash on Delivery) terms. He made a big fuss about that. What he failed to consider is the fact that he had a reputation for lying to get what he wanted. He paid his bills only when there was some sort of grave consequence to him if he didn't. He paid the people first whom he needed next and so forth. No doubt, the guy was a scoundrel.

After several phone calls, I did not relent on my insistence on COD. I rescinded my quotation altogether.

I then received yet another call from this disgruntled fellow who absolutely could not believe that I was refusing to do any business with him. He point blank asked me why. This is what I told him: "One time you sold your integrity, and as far as I am concerned you can't get it back. You have a reputation for hurting people. I am not interested in doing business with you. I will never allow you to owe me any money."

He was absolutely in disbelief that I would pass up the opportunity to make a buck. What he did not seem to understand was that my integrity was simply not for sale at any price. I had my standards and he did not measure up. I have not heard from him since.

Here is the lesson: Your integrity is an asset to be guarded with passion. It will see you through difficult times. If for some reason you compromise it, repent and hope for forgiveness but don't expect it. And above all don't make anyone else responsible for your screw-up.

At Weiland Doors, the only thing we have to sell is service. In any successful business that is the absolute foundational element. Every aspect of that business should be centered on serving the customer as well as possible.

That customer can never be served if he or she is not dealt with in a forthright manner. Whether or not the answer to the question is what the customer wanted is secondary to whether or not it is truthful.

For me, there is nothing that will cause me to end a business relationship faster, or any relationship for that matter, than the feeling I am being "jacked around." I simply will not tolerate it.

A few years ago a potential customer called me from North Carolina. We had a conversation in which we discussed his door requirements. I agreed to give him a quotation, which turned into a purchase order from him. Our typical terms at that time were to give a 2 percent discount for payment in ten days, or net thirty days if the discount was not taken.

Before agreeing to extend non-COD terms, I had my administrative associate, Terry Price, check out his credit because I sensed he was a scoundrel. There was something in his voice that did not set right with me. We checked out his credit. It all came back finer than frog hair. We extended the terms. He paid on time.

Sometime later he again ordered a couple doors and paid on time. The fourth order from him was a $42,000 contract. This time he did not take the discount and did not pay on time. I wrangled with him for over eight months, getting paid a little at a time.

Once during all those conversations, I stated to him, "Bill, you continually lie to me. Why?" He went on to give me some song and dance about how a businessman should understand that sometimes lying is necessary to stay in business.

After finally receiving final payment on that fiasco, I never spoke with him again. A couple years later the folks who employed him to install doors in their plant informed me he was no longer in business. I wasn't surprised.

I have returned to that first conversation from time to time. My first hunch was that he was not to be trusted. I was right. It has been my experience that there is something in the voice of a scoundrel that is common to that ilk. I have never exactly been able to put my finger on it. Whether it's a word misspoken, unwanted flattery, omitted facts, it is difficult to define. But deception is there to be sure.

There was another guy from Idaho who, out of the clear blue sky, called me with a door request. I am always suspicious when I get a request like this. I always wonder who they haven't paid. Most likely, when things are going well, people tend to go down the same road. There are not that many specialty door manufacturers; they can be counted on one hand. There are none of them in my opinion who do a horrible job of making doors, so one needs to ask if the customer is doing a horrible job of paying them.

Again the company's credit checked out okay. So we went ahead with the sale, never forgetting my suspicions. This guy paid all right. He just took ninety days to do it. He was always thankful about how well we worked with him.

After a handful of sales he sent us a quote request totaling over $80,000. I returned the quote with a note at the bottom that the sale would require half the money with the order and half prior to shipping. I never heard from him again.

It was my suspicion that this guy was setting me up for the big hit. He obviously did not have the money or the credit to obtain it. Either way I did not want to do business with him. He seemed to want me to be his banker but he didn't tell me so. I am not a banker. I'm a door manufacturer. So I ended our relationship.

I always like to do business with people who make a lot of money and who have a lot of money. This is why. In business, things inevitably go wrong. Sometimes people make mistakes. Those with the money will fix it. Those without it will leave you holding the bag.

A few years ago a rather large food processing company went bankrupt, owing one of my customers a quarter of a million dollars. My customer had not been in business long enough to absorb this kind of loss. He became slow at paying but always forthright. We went along with him for the time it took him to get back on his feet. One day he was thanking me for my patience with him.

I simply said, "I would rather do business with an honest man who was having difficulty paying than with a crook who paid his bills on time." An honest man will somehow find a way to pay you, but a crook will find a way not to.

> *Here is the lesson: While I'm talking with potential customers, I am constantly monitoring how I feel during the conversation. If I get that funny feeling in my stomach, it sends up a red flag to watch out. Sometimes I point blank surprise them with this question, "Are you going to pay me?" If they hesitate even a split second, the deal is off. Scoundrels don't like that question. They always hesitate. Doing business with a crook is like dealing with a time bomb. You may get away with it for a while, but if you do it long enough, he will find a way to abscond with your money. It's just a matter of time. Be careful!*

Completely on the other hand was Jerry Woods. He owned a successful industrial insulation business. As his company would erect insulated panel walls for the food industry, he purchased Weiland Doors to install in those walls. His integrity was second to no one I knew. When he spoke, you could take it to the bank. He, along with a handful of others, was instrumental in the early success of Weiland Doors.

I remember taking a short business trip with him to a meat processing facility in west central Iowa back in the days when I knew nobody and Jerry knew everybody. It was my deal we were after, but he insisted on driving.

At that time I drove an old Ford Taurus that Al Pfeifer, Jean's first cousin, had constructed from two wrecked cars. Al owned a body shop in Madison. When business was slow, he would buy wrecked cars and repair them for sale at a discounted price. This Taurus was one of those cars.

It was a decent car except that anyone following it down the road had to notice it kind of ran in a dog-leg fashion. In other words the back wheels did not run in the same tracks as the front wheels. Maybe that's why Jerry insisted on driving, but I doubt it.

Jerry came from the same side of town as I did. He never forgot where he came from and reminded me often to do the same. The exercise of remembering where I began has a way of keeping me thankful and humble. It has been proven time and time again that this was vital part of a great platform from which to launch any business.

As I slid into the front seat of his new Cadillac, I was impressed to say the least. I had never ridden in such a beautiful automobile. It still had the smell of new leather seats and was spotless. I commented on how nice it was. Jerry replied that I would be driving one of these too someday. Back then I was still concentrating on just putting food on the table for our seven-member family. Driving a new Cadillac certainly seemed remote.

As we drove to our destination, I couldn't help but feel at ease. Jerry had a way about him that I have always admired. He made whoever he was with feel important. I don't remember much else about the drive.

When we arrived at the plant, I couldn't help notice that this guy knew everyone's first name. I could tell they loved him. Not only that, he loved them. As we walked through the plant, he spoke to virtually everyone and he flattered no one. His comments were absolutely genuine. I could feel it. Jerry brightened every room he entered. It was no wonder he was such a business success. Folks loved doing business with Jerry Woods, and I did too. He was one of my heroes. Much of my success can be attributed to his wonderful example.

The saying that Weiland Doors only sells service was gleaned from Jerry Woods. But what is it that people want and need almost more than anything else? If you answer this with any number of "things" people spend their life endeavoring to acquire, you are wrong. After food and water, the next thing they need is to be appreciated, to be important, to be cared for, and to be loved. With that premise we can provide the absolute most wonderful products available and go broke doing it.

You see, folks want to be given what Jerry Woods offered to everyone he met that day. Why wouldn't he be welcome wherever he went? He gave the folks what they needed. For some of them his friendly demeanor may have been the brightest spot in their day.

Here is the lesson: In business people will overlook your weaknesses if they like doing business with you. And that will happen if you help them feel like the important people they actually are. Treating them in a friendly, respectful, and forthright manner is the way that's done. A thankful attitude for the folks who put the bread on the tables of everyone in your company will go an incredibly long way.

I have modeled my business after the way I was inspired to do so. In the beginning Weiland Doors were rather crude in their design. But by using Jerry's example, that crudeness was overlooked time and time again. It allowed me to stay in the game until I could come out with better and better designs. It allowed me to provide for my family in ways I never would have been able to had I provided only the doors. The integrity I exhibited to my customers was paramount to my success.

Six hundred people attended my father's funeral. We hardly had enough room for them all. They came to pay their respects to a man they held in high esteem for his virtues of honesty and integrity. Regardless of the problems my father may have had communicating with his own family, in the community of Madison, he was a man of integrity.

Nowhere in life is integrity more important than in marriage. It seems to me entering into a marriage relationship most likely is the biggest business deal any of us will ever encounter. A lapse in integrity could very well cause you to lose half or more of what you might consider all your assets, not to mention your spouse and your children.

The business of marriage and raising children is the toughest business I've encountered in my life. It requires delicate decisions and social skills beyond any that are required anywhere else. The emotion involved in many family decisions is astronomical, making them even more difficult. Even at that, if ever life depended on good choices, this is where that needs to happen.

Difficult choices abound. Sometimes parenting requires tough love. As parents, Jean and I never allowed our children to watch PG-13 movies—at least not when they lived in our house. This wasn't easy on them when they heard from other kids at school what they were missing because we didn't subscribe to HBO or Cinemax. But after a while, they learned not to care what everyone else was watching. Instead, they watched what was morally healthy and listened to motivational speakers, especially while we were traveling in the car. We wanted them to be affected by the good, the clean, the pure, and the powerful. They turned out just fine.

To this day they sometimes expound on the value of those lessons and do whatever they can to be sure their children are influenced positively in the same way. We have been told by our adult children how proud they are of our courageousness as parents and how we guided them away from negative influences and toward positive ones.

Teaching integrity involves more "doing" than it does "saying." You can harp to your kids all day about the importance of not lying, cheating, or stealing, but if they don't see you practicing what you preach, how much weight do your sermons really carry?

When our children were young, I bought a camper for vacations. I bought a camper because we had five young children, and fire codes in hotels don't allow you to have seven people staying in one room. I wasn't able to afford two hotel rooms and was unwilling to lie to the hotel clerk when checking in and being asked how many people there were in our party. Other people might not have even blinked an eye at this gesture, but I simply couldn't lie to a proprietor who had every right in the world to decide the rules and regulations of his establishment.

When we'd go to amusement parks or restaurants, I'd also be completely honest about the ages of the children. They were petite in stature, so I could have lied about how old they were to save a few bucks on kids' meals, but it was simply not in my character to do such a thing.

These are small gestures in the grand scheme of things, but they're also essential in the character formation of children. Our children saw my example and as they aged I am proud they have acquired the same level of integrity as they were taught.

Consider that million-dollar whore. For that kind of money, what would you do? What would you do to save the cost of a hotel room or $100 a day at Disney World? Do you cheat on your income taxes? Where is your threshold of whether or not you become dishonest? Not having a threshold is good. If you do, how are you different from the two people negotiating the deal at the beginning of this chapter?

18

POVERTY IS A THINKING PROBLEM ... IN THE U.S.

As a youth I was no different than any other kid. I liked to hang out with people close to my own age. Mike Mazuch and I were born on the same day in the same hospital and lived less than a mile apart throughout our childhood. We didn't associate much during our elementary school years because we went to different schools. Mike attended the public school, and I, a Catholic boy, went to St. Leonard's.

In 1963 when the Nebraska State Legislature introduced rural busing, Mike and I became friends as we rode the same school bus. Mike's dad, Bill, was our bus driver.

As farm neighbors, the men exchanged help on jobs that were more labor intensive. Shelling corn was one of those jobs. However, as my dad owned the corn sheller, he could not take part in the work of pulling the corn from the crib because he was needed to run the machine. In order to do his neighborly part, he supplied a man to help in his place.

The summer when I was fourteen, I finally got the chance to prove I was physically big enough to do that job. So in the afternoon heat with the chaff spouting out of the dried ear corn, I proved that a strapping youth could do the job of any man when it came to busting his tail on a corn hook (the tool used to rake the corn out of the crib).

After the crib was empty that day, Art Zessin, another neighbor, returned from delivering a load of corn to the Farmer's Elevator. Before leaving town he had stopped off at the local tavern to pick up beer and soda for all the workers. As Mr. Zessin passed out the beer to the adults, Bill Mazuch simply stated, "I'll have a Pepsi. Thanks."

At the time I thought that to be a rather peculiar request: a grown man having a soda when all the other men were having a beer. In the forty some years since that incident I have never forgotten it. Why didn't he have a beer just like everyone else? I never asked and he gave no explanation

That simple gesture by Bill taught me a lot that day. Bill demonstrated in his quiet, calm manner that it was okay to do something different than the crowd. To me, a teenager, it was a remarkable statement. I remember it as if it was yesterday.

I have always been somewhat of an odd thinker. It is not my nature to give much consideration to the opinion of others. I don't think Mr. Mazuch had any great effect on my thought progression; however, I do think he substantiated that the unique ways in which I think and express my thoughts are just fine.

I once read a statement in the John Deere monthly publication *Furrow Magazine*, "One would care a whole lot less about what others thought if it was considered how little time they spent doing it." I don't know for sure how much truth there is to that statement. However, I do suppose there is some. Anyway I think it is somewhat interesting to consider.

In 1996, Thomas J. Stanley and William D. Danko shed some light on wealth in America in their award-winning book *The Millionaire Next Door: The Surprising Secrets of America's Wealthy*. Millionaires don't think in the same manner as most. They are different.

Stanley and Danko pointed out some of the key characteristics found in millionaires—true millionaires—and they elaborated on the behavioral patterns of these select few who account for a majority of the country's personal wealth. I've found some patterns in the behavior and mindset of millionaires myself, which are probably best exemplified in a phrase I like to use: "Millionaires think like millionaires." If they thought like everyone else, they wouldn't be.

Let's clarify something here. There are those in this country in the position of having tremendous amounts of financial resources, but who have little or no appreciation of how it was acquired. They have what might be called "Paris Hilton Syndrome." These people just have it. In no way have they acquired it. Because of this I exclude them from that group of folks who have, because of their own savvy, become wealthy.

For a long time I have believed poverty is not a money problem. It is rather a thinking problem. I do not think this to be true in many countries of the world. In many, especially developing countries, there is simply little or no opportunity to raise one's self from the cycle of poverty in which the masses of people find themselves. The Stanley/Danko book only examined characteristics of people living in the U.S. So when I state that poverty is a thinking problem and not a money problem, I am referring to the U.S population.

I don't mean that all millionaires think exactly alike, but they do approach life in a manner that's different from the rest of the populace. For example, I've never once heard one talk of winning the lottery as a way to acquire wealth.

True millionaires don't rely on the pure happenstance of a lottery ticket to make money. They instead rely on patience, intellect, and decisiveness. After all, a millionaire has the same chance of winning the lottery as any John Doe who doesn't possess one ounce of that which is essential to become wealthy. There's no skill involved in winning the lottery. All you need is a dollar and you're on the same playing field as a hundred million other people with hopes set on striking it rich with a lucky ticket.

I have never in my life bought a lottery ticket. It is my opinion that gambling is a tax on poor people, even if they are willing participants. I have been in the grocery line too many times when a rag-tag person in front of me plops down a $20 for cigarettes and lottery tickets.

I simply have too much compassion to agree with laws that allow the weakness in my fellow man to be exploited. We live in a society that glamorizes wealth without defining it. Again it has little to do with money and much to do with the way one thinks. Promoting the idea that purchasing cigarettes and lottery tickets will lead to anything but poverty is a huge lie that far too many have believed.

Even though I know that the wealthy purchase lottery tickets as well, it is done more for entertainment and without any belief that they will ever be a winner. They'd rather tilt the odds in their favor by seeking out business opportunities that best fit their individual skill sets and strengths.

During his working life, my dad accumulated an estate that would certainly cause him to be considered a wealthy man. He didn't think the same way as the rest of crowd. He thought like the millionaire he was. I'm not sure where he developed that line of thinking, but he thought this way as far back as I can remember.

When I was in grade school, my dad drilled me on my multiplication tables. He made me memorize and recite them from two to fifteen. He also drilled me on fractions, making sure I could convert fractions into percentages in my head instantly. I can still remember that one-seventh is a little more than 14 percent. I never understood why he was so insistent that I was able to do this mental math, because I didn't see other kids' dads drilling them with arithmetic, so I asked him once why he made math such a priority.

He gave me this lesson: As a farmer my dad was a cattle feeder. He bought 400-pound calves in the fall, which he fed and cared for until they were market ready sometime within the following year. He could fairly well determine the cost of growing the cattle from 400 pounds to 1,200 pounds. However, he had no way of knowing how much he would receive for them at the end of their growth period.

The one thing he had control over was what he paid for them. Cattle were sold at auctions. At those auctions a group of calves would be brought in. Once in the auction ring the buyers had to make extremely quick decisions on how much they were willing to pay; these were decisions that would affect their financial bottom line a year later. Those decisions in no way could be made doing math using a pencil and paper. (There were no calculators at that time.) They were made by mentally running the numbers; it simply required doing the math in your head.

My dad taught me how to think fast and on my feet. He knew that if I was to be financially successful, I needed to have the ability to run the numbers quickly.

That was my dad's world. He knew the importance of being self-reliant and thinking fast. He knew that if a man was to survive as a farmer, many times he had to think quickly and accurately because there was no way to escape the consequences of bad decisions.

It didn't matter that none of my friends' dads drilled them with multiplication tables. He was going to make sure that I knew mine. I am proud of him for giving me this gift. This ability has always been beneficial in enabling me to be successful far beyond anything I had imagined not that many years ago.

I mentally run the numbers as a first step in almost any decision I make. How much does it cost? Can I afford it? And is it worth the risk? The correct answers to these questions are absolutely necessary if one wants to be financially successful.

My dad and I have always possessed characteristics of an entrepreneur, but being one isn't for everybody. We seem to have a greater tolerance for uncertainty. There exists a great likelihood of periods of much work with little pay. However, the excitement of the whole operation, and its potential, is simply too hard to ignore.

The name "cowboy" comes to mind when describing folks with the independent spirit of virtually all the entrepreneurs I've known. Folks of this sort tend not to follow the social norms when it comes to financial matters. Thinking outside the box is more in conformity with the way they are.

True millionaires that I know aren't pretentious as they're so often characterized. What you see with these people is usually what you'll get.

A couple years ago I was shopping for a new car for Jean. I test drove several, including a new Lexus. During the drive I relayed to the sales lady that I thought it was important to consider my standing in the community when buying a new automobile. I then asked her if she knew what the most popular vehicle was among millionaires. She paused a bit and answered, "A Lexus?"

I responded, "Oh no, madam, they drive Ford F-150 pickup trucks. Folks who drive Lexuses tend to not have near that much money because they blow it on things to make themselves look rich when they can't afford it."

I did not buy that Lexus. They are no doubt fine automobiles, but I decided not to afford what they cost.

Please note what I said here. I decided not to afford; I could have, but I bought Jean a shiny new red Cadillac with all-wheel drive for thousands less. She didn't ask for such a nice car but I got her one anyway. She was happy and so was I.

And by the way, I paid cash. I don't know any millionaires who slave away working so they can make payments on a car that is way beyond their means. All that silliness has its consequences. Many times it comes when the person needs to retire for some reason or other and can't afford to.

In 2009 I was diagnosed with chronic leukemia. That along with my age has required me to adjust my lifestyle. I am glad for the financial decisions we made over the last thirty years, which have given me the luxury to do that. I simply have not had the energy to do what I once did. That's usually the case with the wealthy; they don't rely on credit to provide them with a façade of wealth. If they use credit at all, they use it as a tool to leverage their position with a sound business strategy.

We're a country that operates on a huge line of credit and has its citizens believing that the American dream is easily attainable thanks to this glorious device. Please don't misunderstand me here. I think this country is the greatest country on earth, but it's also a country where everything from a new car to a $30 desk lamp can be purchased with credit and delayed payment options.

This ideology is so pervasive today that anyone who doesn't think in such terms is considered an anomaly. And those are your typical wealthy, always running the numbers on whatever venture they're undertaking and constantly weighing the pros and cons of every situation. In that respect, they are an anomaly. These are calculating people with calculating ways of thinking. They do not make many financially inept decisions!

The word *luck*, I believe, has much to do with things over which I have little or no control; the country in which I was born, my level of intelligence, my looks, my parents' social status and the like. On the other hand what many think of as luck is not luck at all, but instead it is no more than an opportunity prepared for. That is my definition anyway.

Once a guy told me he wished he were as lucky as I was. If he were, then supposedly his wife could stay home and not have to work a job.

I never responded. Even with my medical issues and age, that guy would have had a heart attack if he followed me around very long. He liked to have fun. He and his wife attended all the local ballgames, attended the Huskers games on Saturdays during the fall, played golf two nights a week. All the while I worked at my own game—calculating the risks, running the numbers, and flat out-working most everyone else.

You're darn right I'm lucky—not by his definition, but by mine.

I drive by the golf course regularly. I never could figure out what all the fuss was about. My game was and is a whole bunch more exciting, and it returned to me what many of those folk out there wanted but didn't have whatever it took to get out there and get it. When the deal was in front of me, I saw it because I was prepared and acted. I love working, always have. In that game I have won time and time again.

I have encountered situations when dealing with governmental agencies in which the rules were unclear or perhaps I was unaware a rule even existed. Several times I have found myself in those situations. I have found more success in asking for forgiveness than permission. When asking for permission, there's the tendency for the grantor to self-inflate their political importance and respond with a resounding no. Requesting permission, even though it is sometimes necessary and important, is empowering the person whose critical affirmation might be required to answer in the negative.

I suggest, instead, proceeding. If a problem raises its head high enough to demand attention, go to those same people and ask for forgiveness, but only if you are reasonably sure you have at least some ground to stand on. What I believe you are doing in this case is empowering the other to respond in the typical self-centered way, only in the opposite direction. People tend to want to be important, and what is more important than owning and distributing forgiveness? You will very likely get what you require.

Several years ago I hired a contractor to build a deck and screen porch on my lake house. Before commencing that project I inquired of my neighbors if they had any objection. None did, so we began.

One day the building inspector drove by our house and noticed I was building the deck within twelve inches from the property line. I was soon to find out that a building permit was required. Since we were replacing an existing deck and since the contractor had not applied for a permit, I never gave considerable thought to the necessity of acquiring one.

This guy who holds the "awesome responsibility" of giving out building permits put a stop on the project right then and there and threatened me with a stiff fine if I proceeded without a permit, and informed me that I needed to make an application. The application process included written permission from my neighbors and several copies of drawn plans that described the project in detail. In addition I would need to reconcile the issue with the lake association building committee.

After compiling the necessary documents, I was required to appear before the building committee to explain the situation. I simply stated I was "just dumb" and asked that they forgive my ignorance of the rules. They asked a few questions and approved my project unanimously.

Now if, on the other hand, I would have approached the same situation in an arrogant manner, by complaining about how much authority they had and the ways they used it, I doubt they ever would have given me permission to continue building the deck. That same evening a young attorney and his wife approached that same board fifteen minutes before us using bully tactics. They were rewarded with quite the opposite response.

Remember, if people like you, they'll seek out ways to help you and do business with you.

Being a millionaire is about a mindset, a mentality. You can't be afraid of work and you can't be afraid to think differently.

A positive self-concept also plays a large role in the mind of a millionaire. I'm not talking about gung-ho bravado, but an innate belief that you're capable of doing whatever it is you're doing. Business, after all, is right between your ears. Whether your business is manufacturing, selling, or teaching, you've got to believe you have goods to get the job done. If you can't convince yourself of the value of your product, how can you possibly convince anyone else?

A good salesperson is convinced of the value of his product. He knows that the person who can list everything that's wrong with a product is, in fact, ripe for a sale. It's likely to sell more to a person who can tell you everything wrong with a product than one who just says, "I don't care." The one who's rattled off the list of complaints has at least done his homework and researched the product. I believe challenges can be responded to in one of two ways. You can either let the challenge bury you emotionally or physically, or you can rise up and meet it head on.

As you might imagine, being the cowboy that I am, I'd much rather meet a challenge head on. Challenges are like fences, and cowboys would much rather do whatever it takes to get around the fence—whether that means leaping over it or crawling under it—than let it keep them from achieving their goals.

Numerous times in my life I've gone through periods where challenges nearly broke me emotionally. Certainly my early years spent going broke was one of those times. The emotional weight of such a challenge is enough to make any man want to just lie down and go to sleep, buried under a rock of emotional chaos. But those are just the times when the millionaire inside all of us, the person inside ourselves who says *you can do this*, rises up and keeps going. It's not easy. In fact, it's flat out hard work. But it's how you respond to such chaos that counts.

As I get older, I find myself relying more on my intellect and less on my raw energy to respond to challenges. My body parts seem to be wearing out and that, along with this chronic leukemia, has made physical activity more and more challenging. But my intellect hasn't left me, nor has my desire to respond to the challenges staring me in the eye. Remember, the body can bring to fruition what the mind can seize.

Financial wealth is not that elusive in this country. It takes time, perseverance, and sound decision making. It is not the lottery; the odds are much better than that.

Several years ago I began using the term *cosmic reality* to describe things that just were. For instance the harder a ball is thrown at the floor, the harder it will bounce. Good cause, good effect; bad cause, bad effect; and so forth.

If you smoke, there is a 100 percent chance you will develop unwanted physical symptoms. How insane is it to smoke and hope not to be sick?

A comedy show on TV years ago portrayed a doctor standing by the front desk in his office while a patient would come running in saying, "Doc, Doc, it hurts when I do this." And the doctor would exclaim, "Well then don't do that."

How often do folks make the same type of ridiculous claims? If you throw the ball through the window, it is going to break the window. And furthermore someone will need to sweep up the glass, and it may as well be you. It seems to me none of this is difficult to understand. Going through life with little thought and no plan will yield little in the form of financial security.

Here is the lesson: Someone once told me, "If you do what you do, you will get what you got." I think this is a sound and simple rule. If you are dissatisfied with the direction of your life, change. When using the telephone, if you dial the same number, do you expect a different party to answer? Hello? How is this any different?

19

OFFENSE–DEFENSE

Just like in any game, the business of money management requires offense and defense. If you expect to win the game, you've got to manage both sides of it. It's difficult to improve your financial status if you only do one or the other.

When I was a child, our family knew another farm family that seemed to practice only one side. My dad often explained how Ed and Elaine weren't doing so well. It seemed no matter how hard Ed worked, his wife blew the money on silly stuff they couldn't afford. And for some reason many times Ed couldn't get the hay bales picked up from the field until they were rotten and moldy, which was poor fodder for the milk cows that provided their family sustenance.

In the end they sold the farm that Elaine had inherited from her parents. This really bothered my dad. It seemed to him they were going in the opposite direction he was.

Even at that Dad never missed an opportunity to explain why he was doing well while another guy was going broke. In the case of Ed and Elaine they simply did not defend what they and Elaine's family had accomplished.

Quite the opposite were three bachelors who lived down the road a couple miles from our farm. Together they purchased numerous farms during the 1930s when farms were being sold for the taxes. Throughout those hard years they somehow not only kept their farms together, they acquired more while many of their counterparts lost theirs.

These guys played defense like no one else. They lived in a wood-heated shack with no running water and discarded newspapers covered the window panes to keep out the winter cold. They never married, thereby saving the expense of having a family. They shared a thirty-year-old automobile that doubled as their farm truck. The soles of their shoes were fastened to the leathers with recycled baling wire. They wore their bib overalls for weeks at a time without washing them to save water and soap. The ribs of their cows, who licked holes in the ground where alkali deposits provided them salt, could be counted from lack of food to minimize feed costs. Yet they subscribed to the *Wall Street Journal,* which they read faithfully. All this happening twenty to thirty years after the Depression ended.

I recall overhearing a conversation between my father and the oldest of these three brothers. Because he had been sick, he had reluctantly gone to see a doctor. After a battery of tests, he was prescribed a heart pacemaker. This left him in a tizzy about what to do. The pacemaker was going to cost him a wad of money. I remember him asking my dad if he thought they were worth money.

HELLO! Even as a teenager I thought, "What? You're going to die without one! Put the darn money in your caskets and see if it's worth anything on the other side." Now that's defense.

The 1930s left many farmers with the ability to play monetary defense just like our neighbors. Many of them, whether they survived financially intact or having lost everything, never emotionally recovered. They simply could not adjust to better times; instead, they continued to live as if their very lives depended upon defending their assets.

The brothers died one by one, leaving their assets to the surviving brothers or brother as it were. When the last one died, their relatives fought over the division of what they had given so much to preserve.

> *Here is the lesson: Virtually all of the people scarred by the Great Depression are no longer alive. With them died a valuable experience. In this country more and more people are subscribing to the notion of getting something for nothing. If this trend continues, it would seem to me, anyway, the time will come when the ones who are willing to work for what they have will simply be unable to bear the burden of feeding the balance of the population who, for one reason or another, have ascribed to the idea that they are entitled to have a portion or all of their livelihood for free. There is ample history to support my thinking. If you are young and buying into this minimalist concept, get ready to be hungry. The time could come when no one will feed you. And why should they?*

For farmers during the 1930s there was no offense. There was no money to be made. In fact, there simply wasn't any money.

My father was the first person I knew who worked the offense well in addition to fabulous defense.

I remember an incident in the barn when I was about twelve years old and still thought my dad knew everything. I was helping him vaccinate some little pigs. He was telling me about his views on life. I remember him saying that to be successful and get ahead it was necessary to "think big."

My dad was born in 1927, not long before the drought and Depression of the 1930s. He experienced growing up as a sharecropper's son.

By the time he was my age of twelve, his family had lived on three different rented farms. I do not remember my father ever telling me why this had happened. However, because of the way he spoke of the experience, it must have been traumatic. What I do know is that we lived on the same rented farm until I was a junior in high school when my dad bought that 160-acre rented farm for $46,400—cash.

That was the second time he had done that. In about 1960 he purchased another 160-acre farm adjacent to that one for $24,000—a cash deal as well.

On that first farm was a large beautiful home, much bigger and nicer than the one we lived in. However, it was in need of upgrading, and he wasn't willing to part with the money for which he had other plans. Dad rented it out a couple times and became thoroughly disappointed with the quality of people who were willing to live there as it was.

After a couple years, he let it sit vacant and in disrepair. Occasionally it was used as storage space for soybean seed held over to plant the next year's crop. To him that was a far better use of the building than rental property. Remember, my dad didn't think like everyone else.

On the rented farm where we lived, my dad played his game. When he and Mom moved there shortly before I was born, the fields were infested with noxious weeds. Cockleburs and sunflowers were rampant. Dad knew that a long-term stay on that farm would require getting them in check.

In the summer heat he chopped and hoed weeds while they were small and seedless. When they matured to the point of bearing viable seeds, he carried the plants to the edge of the cornfield where he loaded them on a hayrack for transfer to the burn pile, where the plants along with their noxious seeds were destroyed. He kept up this regimen, so as the years went by those weeds became scarce.

I don't know of another man who ever accomplished this feat with a hoe and machete. If you haven't experienced the intense summer heat of a Midwestern cornfield, I doubt you can truly appreciate what he did. The personal grit he exhibited in doing this was truly remarkable. He was one tough individual.

Even though he worked incessantly to clean up the fields on that farm, the landowner received 40 percent of the crop. For that reason my dad never expanded his farm to include more and more rented property. Instead he raised livestock and did custom harvesting and corn shelling. In the winter he ran trap lines so he could harvest the furs from muskrat, beavers, raccoons, and an occasional mink, which were sold for cash.

I remember his lesson on this and it was simple: The money earned from these ventures was all his. He wasn't required to share it with the landlord. He cleaned up the farm as a way to defend his ability to play offense.

What a concept and from a man with a ninth-grade education and whose parents never owned the farm.

My dad thought big. His goal was to own his own farm so he would never be forced to move—and build a new home. He did both by the time he was forty-one.

Obvious to me, achieving your financial goals is very important. However, along with this it would seem there needs to be personal goals. Goals I don't know if my father ever considered. He seemed to be so focused on his gig that he failed to consider the needs of the other members of his family. He flat out overworked his sons, I being one of three, to the point of sometimes hating him.

His thoughts and goals were developed as a child of the thirties. Even though he was a religious man, food and money, it seemed, were everything to him.

I was a child of the 1950s and 1960s where things were pretty good. As a teenager my need was to play sports and hang out with my high school friends. Conversely, as a teenager my dad's goals were to earn money to have enough food and maybe a little spending money. Against that backdrop his relationships with his sons were stormy at best.

Several years ago at a technology workshop with the public school board, the speaker announced that our children's future is not our past. Such wise words!

I have been careful never to pressure my adult children into following in my footsteps. Instead I have encouraged them to have their own goals and gigs.

I have always been proud of the fact that Jean and I were never given anything by our parents. The largest gift we ever received from them was minimal to say the least. What Jean and I have we have earned using our intelligence and the incessant work ethic learned from our parents.

If my children become wealthy, and I hope they will, I want them to be able to prove they did it without parental intervention.

I have heard parents say they just want their children to have a better life than they have had and then proceed to enable them to be less by giving them all this stuff they want, but don't need. Hello! What I hope for my children is the understanding that if they want a better life, it's their responsibility to go out and get it and live with the pride in knowing they did it without me.

The first half of Thomas J. Stanley and William D. Danko's book *The Millionaire Next Door: The Surprising Secrets of America's Wealthy* gives much attention to the habits of millionaires. The second half of the book is about how many of the rich screw up their kids. If I had the choice of growing up under the thumb of my dad versus growing up under some doting parent who gave me everything I wanted, I'll take my dad hands down any day of the week. He was a real SOB at times, but he raised financially responsible adults.

Why is it that so many of today's parents seem to be raising adults who act like children? How much sense does that make?

Like any business, the door business has its ups and downs. During the slow times I continue to work. I have always used these times to get the work done that was difficult to do while business was fast and furious. Slow times allow time to shore up and create relationships with past and potential customers.

During my early years in business there was simply not enough to do in order to utilize all my time. Increasing sales in order to utilize all my time in the shop would have required traveling overnight. But Jean's chronic illness made being away from home impossible. Because of this I was continually trying to make a dollar here or there on some local gig to support our family.

Long before I entered into the door business I purchased a small back-hoe at a farm machinery auction. I intended to resell it and make some extra money. This back-hoe was a tool that mounted on the rear of a farm tractor and was used to dig holes in the ground.

As it were, there was no market for these, so I kept it and made a deal with Percy Resseguie, owner of the local mortuary, to open graves in the local cemeteries. At $200 each, the work allowed me to earn some quick cash in relationship to the time it took to do this. We used this money to provide musical instruments and music lessons for our children. I did this for fifteen years while the children were growing up.

As the door business grew, I no longer had the time required to continue this little venture, so I sold the back-hoe and moved on.

Here is the lesson; When things are going well, it is easy to think it will always be that way. If money is flowing in, it's easy to develop a false sense of security and believe that it'll always be flowing in. On the other hand, when business is slow, you might have a tendency to think just the opposite. These are both pitfalls. Avoid them like the plague. Stay busy and keep working. Use your slow time to develop future business.

There certainly is much to be said about the value of achieving one's financial goals. Sharing those goals, however, is another matter altogether.

Be careful with whom you share your dreams because not everyone will share your enthusiasm. There is something in the human psyche that prevents this from happening. It seems everyone has innate parameters containing their definition of success. It seems when someone in their social circle breaks through those boundaries, all hell can break loose in an attempt to mend the damage. This hell I'm referring to is manifested in gossip, petty jealousies, grudges, ostracism, and the like—none of it positive by any means. I have felt the sting myself and through the experiences of my family, mostly through my children.

As a cattle feeder my dad usually bought heifers to grow in our feedlot. During the fall months, after the crops were harvested, the cattle were allowed to run free on the farm to forage on the crop stubble and small bits of grain left in the field by the harvest equipment.

At this time of year good perimeter fences were required to keep the animals from roaming onto the neighbors' property. However, the fences that typically divide adjacent properties are far from adequate in preventing an amorous bull from making sexual advances to a group of young females destined for the dinner table and not to be mother cows. The best contraceptive in this case would be an eight-foot-tall woven wire bull fence around a small enclosure several hundred yards away from the females.

As it were, our neighbors had a bull, which was not corralled well enough to prevent him from penetrating or scaling the fence separating his property and ours. That bull became a real nuisance.

After several attempts to fix the fence well enough to prevent it from being compromised, Dad decided to have a conversation with the neighbor about the problem. I went along for the ride and to help out in the event they agreed to round up the bull and pen him in a small enclosure in his farmyard.

After a few sentences of small talk, Dad broached the subject of the bull. The words were no more out of his mouth when the neighbor cut loose with a tirade of how my dad was nothing more than "a big shot cattle feeder who was only interested in lording it over his neighbors." This tirade went on for several minutes. My dad was silent in disbelief, as was I.

The outburst had nothing to do with the bull. Rather it was only about this guy's petty jealousies and grudges toward my dad for being successful.

My dad finally said some things to help him settle down and somehow the bull problem was worked out.

However, the bull problem was not the issue I wish to zero in on here. I have never forgotten the neighbor's response. It had absolutely nothing to do with the problem, but he used it as an opportunity to verbally attack my father for breaking through the boundaries of his definition of success. All hell did break loose that day.

All through our children's school years they continually had difficulties for this same reason. And it was not just our children; it was all the kids who aspired to excellence. Whether it was in academics or sports, it was the same over and over again. They felt the sting of breaking through those social parameters.

As a high school junior, one of my daughters was having a particularly difficult time as the starting point guard on the varsity basketball team. Girls can be catty and backstabbing unlike the neighbor who came right out with his pettiness. In desperation one day she asked one of the other players why they were giving her so much grief. The answer was that she simply worked so hard. Again someone, my daughter, had broken through the boundaries.

Achievement typically involves accepting some resentment of others. Thinking big, as my father described it, will many times be a night-and-day difference from the thinking of others.

I have come to the conclusion that jealousy is one of the foundational issues affecting small towns. I don't believe there is anything else having a more negative effect on the growth of small communities in rural America.

One hundred years ago small towns were being settled across the country, one after the other. For the towns to be successful, everyone settling there needed each other to pitch in and help the common good. Everyone had a common fate because the success of the town rested on each person's shoulders. But as these towns matured, people began to depend on their neighbors less and less, and competition developed among them.

This happens everywhere, not just in small towns, but the main difference is that in large cities you can move several miles to a different neighborhood while still being in the same town. In rural communities moving several miles means leaving town.

There are many advantages to living in small town America. Why is it that so many young people choose to move elsewhere?

Many people would contend there are no jobs other than low paying and factory jobs. This begs the question as to what is the driving force in creating jobs, any jobs. I contend it is the smallest of small businesses.

What type of personality is it that digs those little businesses out of the ground in the first place, with maybe nothing more than a rock, a club, hope, and a dream? They are none other than the sons and daughters with an entrepreneurial spirit who see what no one else sees and who get their rears kicked by the vast majority who live in fear that their neighbor will challenge their small-minded ideas. The fact that I have never encountered even the suggestion that this is a foundational issue affecting job growth in rural areas, tells me this might very well be true.

The people who write books on these subjects are not part of the crowd who create the jobs. Their thinking cannot be expected to extend beyond their "innate parameters containing their definition of success."

The people who are the butt of this prejudice typically do not hang around long without good cause. Young people, being as transient as they are, rarely do. They take all the innate tools that could be used for the betterment of their communities and move elsewhere. What a loss.

It is my opinion that jealousy kills small towns. I know. I've witnessed it with my own two eyes. I have personally felt its sting.

I ran for election to the local public school board three different times in my life. This was a sobering experience, to say the least. I have a successful marriage to the same woman all my life. We have raised five successful children, all college graduates. I founded a successful national business. I am not a drunk and I have never been in jail. I have lived in this community my entire life.

In all three elections there were three candidates, I being one, to fill three open seats. Which made losing the election virtually impossible. However, in all three elections I received the least amount of votes by a landslide. Even though there were only three people for whom to vote, there obviously were numerous citizens who refused to vote for me. I am convinced the village idiot could have outpaced me in a real election.

Was it because I was incompetent? I doubt it.

When I first volunteered, which is more in line with how I got the job, a local attorney was board president.

We, the board, continued to elect him as such until his term ran out and he declined reelection. At that time the board elected me, the guy with the least amount of votes, the one whom the community at-large had done all in their power to reject. Why did they do that?

A local bank president made it rather clear when he stated I was the only one in the previous election he had voted for because I was the only one he deemed competent to hold the office. The folks who realized the need for competence elected me. The community wanted someone who had not compromised their "innate parameters containing their definition of success."

That same bank president had run for the city council several years earlier. He too had lost by a landslide. We both were reminded to stay in our place and not to upset the community status quo by challenging the conventional thought—thought that is perpetuated by the children born to these adults who accept these same narrow ideas. It's no wonder to me why small towns stay small.

It seems to me that the only thing wealth truly affords is a greater variety of choices. We have all seen the public benefits of those wise choices. On the other hand the opposite is also true. One has to look no further than the Hollywood celebrity circuit to see an example of that. There's an old saying: money is the root of all evil. That might be true; however, it is also the root of a vast amount of good.

Next time you come across a $100 bill, hold it in your hands and sense how it feels. Have you ever heard the term, "Cold, hard cash?" I don't think it is hard or cold. I think it is soft and warm, and the color goes with anything.

Here is the lesson: Keep the money in your hand and use it as a tool for good, because if it ever gets into your heart, you will never get enough. The pain caused by greedy, wealthy individuals is vast. You have to go no further than the 2008 Wall Street meltdown to see the effect.

20

AMERICA THE BEAUTIFUL

Not too long ago, I was standing at a farm equipment dealership service counter waiting my turn to be helped with a broken part for one of my farm implements. As it was they were extremely busy, so one of the people behind the counter summoned the parts manager to help me. I was happy for this extra service so I asked him how things were going.

"Not so good," he said. "I missed two chances."

"What do you mean you missed two chances?" I asked.

"Well, I missed two chances to buy a farm. I should have bought one back in the eighties, but I didn't, and I should have bought one about five years ago, but I didn't do that either."

Then, in great detail, this guy set off on a diatribe about everything that's wrong with the world. Among his gripes and complaints, he mentioned that he thought the price of grain was way too high right now and how this would contribute to the downfall of America.

When he finished, I had to wring my ears of his pessimism. Nothing was right, everything was wrong, and none of it, so he claimed, was his fault.

I had known this particular man since we were both teenagers. He started working at the implement dealer while he was in high school. He worked there through two years of college, and eventually became the parts manager. He has had the same employer for over forty years. He's never aspired to be anything other than the parts manager of this particular farm equipment dealer.

There's certainly nothing wrong with being a parts manager. It's important work. During planting and harvesting seasons his job is paramount to the livelihoods of many farm families. I find his job dedication to be quite admirable. However, I've always been puzzled by how this man thought himself to have such great insights concerning the state of affairs in this country.

Here is the lesson: It seems to me this guy got exactly what he deserved. He stayed out of the game, played it safe, and lamented that he missed the joy of winning. How is it possible to appreciate fully what you have without the risk of losing it? Acquiring what America has to offer or aspiring to something other than the present will require you to risk something you already have. That is as certain as the sun coming up in the morning.

America, by its very design, fosters personal success. The people, resources, and infrastructure are all in place to help people become prosperous. It's all here—we have plenty of food, plenty of cars, hot and cold water running right to our kitchens, heat in our houses, a medical system that's second to none in the world, good security, mass communication, the most sophisticated military in the world to protect us, and airplanes that can fly us anywhere we want to go anytime we want to go there.

We can come and go as we darn well please and nobody's allowed to tell us otherwise. What's so bad about living in America? I just don't see any reason to complain in this country. It's a great place to live.

That isn't to say America has always been that way. I certainly don't want to be hypocritical.

For years, I held that position on the school board in Madison. And during those years, there was a gentleman who sat on the board with me. One time he made a broad statement about how he thought that the height of American civilization occurred during his childhood, the 1950s and 1960s. He expounded on how wonderful it was that the kids' biggest worry during that era was whether to play baseball or go to summer camp.

I took great exception to his remarks. The fifties and sixties weren't so great for me. I had no choices. I did what I was told. Other than going to school, in the winter it was grinding feed for the livestock or pitching manure. In the summer it was hoeing and chopping the weeds from the fields and pasture.

But this guy thought everything was just pure and wonderful. He was so self-absorbed he overlooked the fact that the time period he described was also a time of great unrest and civil disturbance in our country.

For many wealthy families like the one he came from, life probably was great. The mothers all stayed home and raised the children and the fathers went out to earn a living every day. And when the work whistle blew at five o'clock, they all sat around the dinner table and talked about how wonderful everything was.

These glory days were whitewashed even further thanks to television programs like *Leave It to Beaver, Dennis the Menace* and *Father Knows Best,* where parents were all-knowing and uncompromising. Even though I believe these shows to have value in giving families a model to aspire to, I cannot remember one of them addressing racial issues, poverty, or women's inequality or even worse, women's subjugation.

Minority populations during this time period didn't have civil rights systems in place to sustain equality. Many Americans were denied countless jobs and opportunities because of their race.

Women didn't have resources available to them to get out of abusive relationships like they do now. I use the word *subjugation.* This is a strong word. However I saw this submissiveness as I was growing up. Unless you have experienced the unleashing of a Weiland temper, you might not think this possible. One of my second cousins spoke of this behavior rather nonchalantly. He called it "old-school" thinking. Sounds nice but it doesn't soften the blow.

So, for three-fourths of the population in this country, life wasn't so idyllic like my friend on the school board would like to believe. There may be many who remember a wonderful era of America during the fifties and sixties, but that wasn't the America that existed for many. Our country may have looked strong through the lenses of television and radio, but a nation is only as strong as the poorest and most maligned of its ranks.

I think we've come a long way as a country in the fifty or so years since that time. Don't get me wrong, racism is still prevalent and there are still groups of disadvantaged people with a story to tell and nobody to tell it for them, but, for the most part, America has made great strides toward becoming a nation that confronts its civil rights problems rather than ignoring them. Most of the people I deal with on a day-to-day basis don't care what gender a person is or what tone their skin is, but focus rather on the virtues of the person in question.

We Americans have failed miserably in one area. Aborting unborn children is allowed in every state. Even though our laws have granted civil rights to virtually everyone, it has rescinded the rights of any person still living in what should be the safest place anywhere: their mother's womb.

I have struggled with the logical sensibility part of this issue for years. It seems to me that when two people engage in an activity that by its very nature causes the conception of a new human being, destroying that new person is the epitome of child abuse and irresponsibility.

How is it that this horrible and inhuman treatment is allowed to continue? I have heard all the prochoice arguments concerning this issue. I have never heard them broach the subject of child abuse when addressing this issue. It is always addressed as a mother's right to her own body.

It is fair to assert that if one smokes a pack of cigarettes a day, lung cancer or some other malady might be the "unabortable" consequence of such action. Driving without seatbelts might be another. But not sex.

Somehow there seems to be a common opinion that sex is a God-given right so innate that a choice whether or not to participate in it is beyond the realm of possibilities. This being so, there needs to be an escape route via taking the life of another human being.

I see little argument of the existence of behavioral pathology, physical pathology, or mental illness. However, if there was, could their existence be wiped out by a mere vote of the people or a pen strike of the U.S. Supreme Court?

But what if the pathology was never correctly defined, or worse, not defined at all? It seems to me there would be a great deal of chaos if this were to happen. I'm simply proposing the question. Considering the level of sexual irresponsibility seemingly present virtually everywhere, what if not chaos has been caused by the widespread acceptance of contraception and abortion? And if so, might this not be defined as a social pathology? Have we considered the possibility of this?

Have we considered that we may very well be endeavoring to politically and/or judicially eliminate a social pathology, only to find it impossible?

I believe that as a community we are far less by having allowed this line of thought, disguised as prochoice, to continue to exist as normal. Are not children yet to be given birth by their mothers living in a precarious place? Is the danger to them equaled in any other segment of society? If you believe there is, pray tell where?

Here is the lesson: Politically correct thought changes nothing. If there is a social pathology such as I have suggested, denial of its existence will not be sustainable. The truth is what is and it cannot be changed.

We in the U.S. sometimes forget that there is, in fact, an American dream, while people all over the world dream it every day. Allowing foreigners to come into our midst, I believe, causes us to be more appreciative of the gifts we have … and more willing to share.

Wasn't it foreigners who allowed Mary, Joseph, and the Christ Child to live among them in Egypt in protection from King Herod? Could this be a lesson for us?

How can we be so totally consumed in ourselves when the vast majority of the world's population is so destitute? If the celebration of our freedom and prosperity means anything, shouldn't it be about social justice for the masses of people who know of none?

Consider them. They are literally dying to live where we live. Their dream is our reality.

We first met Leysan when she came to the U.S. from Russia on a cultural exchange visa in order to be a nanny for our daughter Stephanie. During the time she was caring for our grandchildren, Stephanie's husband was deployed as he was in the military. Because of this Jean and I visited them about one weekend a month. We became rather attached to Leysan. As her visa was about to run out, we decided to ask her to come with us to

Nebraska and attend college on a student visa. She gladly accepted our offer and became what we refer to her as our Russian daughter.

For the rest of us a bad day in the U.S. is better than most days in other parts of the world. Having Leysan live with us over the past few years has brought that to my attention. When she described her dreams of moving to America at the age of fourteen, I asked her about her emotions when she finally realized that dream by landing in America.

"My first thought was that I'm never going back," she said.

I was touched by how much she cared about coming to America and her willingness to do whatever necessary to stay here. That's why it bewilders me to hear people complain about the lack of opportunity available to them.

We have all heard news stories depicting political corruption in other parts of the world. In many places prosperity is nothing more than a dream, where bone-grinding hard work with little pay is the norm.

Fortunately, as Americans, we're afforded the opportunities to make our lives whatever we want them to be. It's not our birthright, however. It takes determination and hard work. Nothing is new here. If anything has changed it is the number of people who are willing to go the distance to reach their American dream.

21

LIVING WITH GIB!

"Why do you do this to me? Why do you do this to me?" I could hear it already—the lost temper, eyes bulging, screaming with everything he was worth. I knew it was coming.

The spring mud had again plugged the yellow, rusted, narrow front wheels on Dad's Model '44 Massey Harris tractor. It was senseless to clean them because they would be plugged full after driving it another ten feet. In a situation like this, steering the tractor by applying either the right or left rear wheel brake was the only way to control the direction of travel.

It was getting late. Dad, commonly called Gib by nearly everyone, would soon be home from a corn-shelling job. The tension in my head was mounting. By this time I wanted to have the cattle feed ground and in the feed bunks. But instead I had the tractor, with dad's new feed grinder in tow, bogged down in the mud with the drive shaft bent in a 45-degree angle.

The shaft was a telescoping drive line that attached to a splined shaft protruding from the back of the tractor used to power other farm machinery—in this case, a feed grinder.

In my haste I had forgotten to attach this shaft to the tractor as I hitched the grinder to the tractor.

As I rocked the unit back and forth trying to navigate the mud, the back tractor tire caught the loose drive shaft and bent it down in a 45-degree angle. Shortly after Dad drove into the farmyard, and just as I expected, all hell broke loose ... again.

I was fourteen. No amount of sorry ever sufficed for damage like this. The harder I worked at being the perfect kid, the more frustrated I became.

I titled one of the last chapters in my book "Living with a Babe." However, to understand the difficulty I have had doing that, I think it necessary for me to write this chapter first. Some of this was touched on earlier in the book. However, because I did not cover the profound effect my dad's issues of control and abuse have had on the relationships in my life, especially with my wife, Jean, it would seem this is important enough for further consideration.

It has been over forty years since I moved out of my father's house to be in the arms of my loving Jean. I emphasize "loving arms" because it has been the unfailing, tough love of this remarkable woman that has encouraged me to press on.

My father once exclaimed that, "Everything was fine until that damned woman came along." For my dad who had prior to that time always been able to bully his family into submission, those were indeed extremely difficult times.

I understand that many of the folks who knew my father personally will find it difficult to believe some of the things I write about him. He was a respected member of our community. This fact would seem to be substantiated by the hundreds who attended his funeral, many who expounded upon his virtues.

To those unbelievers I simply ask that you consider the seven divorces among my siblings. This fact alone should be evidence enough of the level of dysfunction in the Gilbert Weiland family. After all, we are the ones who lived with him.

Control and abuse typically go together like salt and pepper. You rarely find one without the other, at least not in the more critical situations. In my personal experience control was abuse.

My father like many abusers was a master of deceit. Because they keep such a tight rein on their families, many people have no idea the damage these people do to the people with whom they live. However, you have to go no further than the nearest women's shelter to find out.

I believe for many families there is such a stigma attached to this problem that the very idea of examining it is so painful that it mostly gets swept under the rug and perpetuated onto the next generation.

As I have divulged my father's abusive behavior, I have had responses like, "I can hardly believe that. He was always such a nice guy." They were absolutely right. He was nice to us as well, as long as he got his way.

Have you ever heard the cliché "his way or the highway"? That is not the way it is with abusers. With them it is "his way or all hell breaks loose." The highway is rarely part of the deal. The highway signifies the end of his control.

I use the masculine form when discussing abusers. In my experience, and in the experience of the vast majority, people who do this type of abuse are men. Women, because of their physical size and female temperament, tend not to be the ones who do this to the ones they love.

Let's examine for a moment how controllers think. I have spent forty years overcoming this problem. Believe me, I know this from firsthand experience, from both living with one and subsequently being one.

In healthy relationships the parties grow to love and care for one another. In the normal progression of these relationships, trust in the consistent love of the other makes it possible for love, freely given, to flow between the lovers.

The key words here are *trusted* and *free-flowing*. If that is the basis for normal and healthy, then the basis for abnormal and unhealthy would be just the opposite: suspicious and controlled.

Children raised in chaotic households with skewed or limited boundaries, where love is not trusted but instead manipulated and bartered, tend to become adults who have limited ability to trust that another could actually love them. However, because that love is so absolutely essential to them and since through the actions of another person is the typical way they, or anyone for that matter, feel loved, they attempt to control the actions.

The concept of controlling and extracting love from another might seem bizarre to most. However, to those of us raised in households like mine, it seems absolutely normal. Control, it seems to me, is a recalcitrant personality infection contracted during the formative years of one's life. It becomes an insidious disease that discolors every personal relationship of the one infected and so immense it can rarely be cured but instead only peeled off layer by layer with the hope one might overcome it.

The use of manipulation, intimidation, deprivation, and emotional, physical, and sexual abuse are all common ways abusers use to force the people they love into acting in ways that make them feel loved. They do not do this intentionally. They do it with the same perception as one may have that he or she is walking across the room to answer the phone. Even so, reminding them of their abusive behavior will most likely be interpreted as a personal assault, resulting in more abuse. It takes a strong, determined person to confront this behavior.

When my siblings and I were small children, I think our lives were fairly normal. However, growing into young adults required a change in relationship with our parents. As we matured and began to have thoughts and opinions of our own, Dad saw this as a personal assault. As a result he became more and more controlling as he saw his children growing away from him.

Not only growing away from him, but growing away from each other. One would think that growing up in a family like mine would cause closeness among the siblings. But with no one to pull us together it was everyone for himself or herself. It seems that as children we had limited ability to process all of this.

Because our mother mostly denied what was going on, she was no advocate for us. She mostly was the go between whenever we wanted something from our father. This I believe only enabled his abusive behavior to continue unabated. I never once ever had the experience of having an adult stand up for me. Nor did any of my siblings. We all just took care of ourselves.

In our home and on our farm, everything was about Gilbert Weiland. Any thought or action contrary to his way of thinking was perceived by him as a personal attack, which he countered with a vengeance.

Much of the time during my teenage years he was away tending to his corn shelling or other business, leaving me home to do the farm chores. Even though he rarely worked with me, in so many ways I was expected to know … I stop this sentence short of stating just what he wanted me to know to give you the reader a small sense of the frustration I had with what was required of me. It was usually unclear.

This happened so regularly one would expect I was habitually set up for failure. No matter how hard I tried to figure out what he wanted, if I made a mistake of any kind or broke a piece of machinery, his temper would break loose with an angry tirade. He would scream that same question at me, over and over again, "Why do you do this to me? Why do you do this to me?" He would swear and shame me for being so irresponsible. These sessions would go on until he wore himself out.

He never once apologized for the mental and emotional damage he did. There was a time while I was thirteen or fourteen, like any adolescent, when I just could not seem to keep my mind connected to my body. During this time his verbal abuse was almost a daily occurrence. The more he yelled, the more mistakes I made. I was nauseous much of time along with experiencing severe headaches.

The situation smoothed out as I matured and was for the most part able to do the work without error. By the time I was in my late teens, things were going pretty good for Dad. When I was not in school, I worked morning until dark six days a week. During the periods I was in school, I was not permitted to do any extracurricular activities, but instead was required to come immediately home for livestock chores. If I brought up the idea of playing high school sports, he would shame me for wanting to abandon him.

I was allowed to go out on Saturday night, which was awkward because all my friends played sports and usually there was a game. If there was not a game, they made plans without me simply because I was absent when they made the plans. I adapted and did the best I could.

On Sunday I was allowed to hang out with friends, but again this was difficult. Much of the time what teenagers did back then was just drive around and talk. It was difficult because I was never allowed to do that.

I drove around only once with the family car, a '65 light metallic blue Pontiac Safari station wagon. I did not know that Dad always wrote down the odometer reading. That particular Sunday afternoon I added twenty-six miles to the odometer. Shortly after I returned home Dad checked the odometer. He was livid. He screamed and hollered, accusing me of wearing out his automobile for no good reason. Considering it was eight miles to town and back, I drove his precious automobile eighteen senseless miles.

As usual he got me under control; I never did that again. However, I always felt as if I was mooching from my friends when I rode around with them, so I didn't do much of that either. When I did, they never seemed to mind. Either they had a different sense of justice than that of Gib Weiland or maybe somehow they knew what I was living with. Anyway, I sure had some nice friends.

Even though the abuse and control were extremely prevalent during my teen years, it was apparent during my early childhood years as well, only in a different way. When we were small children, Dad would romp and play with us. We would ride on his back as he bucked and crawled around the house. This was so much fun.

However, for some reason the playing would lead to a tickle session and/or a whisker rub. "Counting our ribs" as he called it began with a burst of laughter and ended with crying and frustration. He simply did not know when to stop. After a few minutes the tickling turned to pain and anger. If we fought back, we were scolded and held down until we stopped acting angry.

The whisker rub amounted to him rubbing stubbly whiskers against our face until it hurt. The outcome was the same as the rib count, more anger and frustration, not to mention the confusion I encountered when my father, on one hand, acted as if he loved me, yet seemed to be hell bent on hurting me.

This happened regularly. As we got older and bigger he stopped doing this to us, however twenty some years later he acted the same with our young children. He learned in no uncertain terms that those activities were not acceptable and would not be tolerated.

There is something about little children and nakedness that seem to go together as beautifully as any gift God ever intended. Any parent of small children has encountered little boys or girls scurrying around in the same attire as the day they were born. I think in most families this is expected and tolerated as a normal activity for a small child.

However, for some reason when my father saw me naked he would snicker and tease me.

I loathed being naked, especially while bathing if he was present in the house for fear he would somehow see. And for good reason. One time in particular he made those snickering remarks upon entering the bathroom to shave while I was taking a bath. I was mortified.

As a five-year-old, I slept on an old single-bed-sized mattress mounted on an expansion spring bed frame in the northwest corner of our old house right next to Mom and Dad's bedroom.

Because we did not have an indoor bathroom, Mom placed a recycled sixteen-ounce tin can under the bed for me to pee in if I woke up during the middle of the night having to go. The problem was that for some reason I didn't wake up. I wet the bed, over and over again. Because Mom only did washing on Monday this caused a considerable problem.

Dad reacted as usual with yelling, shame, threats, and intimidation. None of that helped.

One Sunday my dad's brother, Uncle Bill, and his family came over to our house for a visit. In discussing my bedwetting problem, it was decided to make me wear my peed up underwear on my head while I ran down to the hog shed and back—a round-trip distance of about 100 yards. They actually did this. While this was happening I could hear the adults laughing. My God, that was an awful experience! I do not know when it was that I stopped wetting the bed, but obviously I did.

These behaviors I encountered as a small child were confusing to say the least. There was absolutely no way to deal with the emotional chaos caused by them. Personal boundaries, if they did exist, were constantly moved.

I often wonder if this was the way it was for most kids at that time. Was all this just a product of a different era?

In any event my father's behaviors had a dogged effect as I have dealt with issues, specifically concerning body and sexuality.

From the age of five or six until I was needed to work on the farm, I think he mostly ignored me, which I think was typical of fathers during that time. It was considered their job to earn the money, which by the way he did very well. I have little recollection of interaction with him during this time as long as I behaved myself and didn't cause anyone too much grief.

These were good years. I spent my time daydreaming, teasing my sisters, and building forts with tree bark and discarded rotten lumber. I fed and watered the chickens and delivered cobs to the kitchen.

I'm sure that as a boy I caused my mother a certain amount of torment. I am equally certain that she protected me by relaying little information to my father.

During those years I recall my mother losing her temper at me only once. I was teasing my siblings to a point way beyond what any mother should be required to tolerate. A sibling fight had erupted and I lost my temper. I stomped out of the house while screaming, "I hate you, I hate you!"

As I turned around she was chasing after me with a wire coat hanger. When she caught up with me, I received several well-deserved lashes. I can still remember the determined look on her face as she swatted me.

I think this was counter to her nature. I recall my dad ridiculing her different times for being what he thought was way too lenient on us. There was a family living in the area in which the mother failed to discipline her children. He jeeringly called my mother by that woman's name over and over. My mother's typical way of disciplining us was certainly gentler.

It's ironic that there seems to be little family dysfunction among my mother's (Goodwater) side of the family, which could never be said about the Weilands—the family that my dad used as an example did just fine as well.

My dad loved fishing. Every year we went on one or more fishing trips somewhere. On day trips we would get up early in the morning, do the livestock chores, and off the whole family would go. Since these excursions typically happened on Sunday, our drive would be interrupted so we could attend Sunday Mass. (At that time Saturday evening Mass was not available.)

When we got to the fishing hole, as my dad would call it, everybody who could fish fished. It was expected.

My father was an able fisherman. There were few times when we did not catch a hundred fish or more. Typically we would fish until after dark because, as Dad said, that is when the fish bite best. We would then load up the gear and make the two - to three-hour drive home. Upon arriving we would proceed to clean the fish under the yard light with the mosquitoes biting us as we worked. The rule was if you fished, you were required to hang in there until the work was finished.

On trips where we were gone more than a day, the scenario was mostly the same. The only difference was that some neighbor or relative back home did the livestock chores, which meant the long drive to and from the lake on the same day was not required. This allowed us to fish later into the night, after which all the fish would be butchered and made ready to put in the freezer.

The worst part of this job was contending with the mosquitoes, which were always huge and aggressive. For some reason, though, they did not seem to bite my father. However, they bit through my clothes and left huge welts all over me, especially on my back. Recently my sister, Dianne stated that she had not forgotten incidents such as this because she thought it was so wrong.

In most fishing resorts, the fish cleaning station consisted of a screened-in room with a door similar to a screened-in porch. This prevented the mosquitoes from entering. However, at the one where we typically stayed, the screens were ripped and the door was missing. It was in a sorry state of disrepair.

Once, when we were unable to stay at this place, we stayed at a place down the lake-shore where everything was tidy and in order. It was heavenly. The cabins, along with the cleaning station, were repaired and working. But with that came a higher price Dad was unwilling to pay unless he had to. The next time we stayed in the same broken-down place as usual, and as usual the mosquitoes were abundant.

To overcome the drudgery, I timed over and over how long it took to completely process one fish. I became so efficient that I could ready a fish for the frying pan in less than a minute. I consider this a victory in making the best of a tough situation for a boy.

The last time I went on a fishing trip with my family was during the summer after my eighth-grade graduation. Big Stone Lake in west central Minnesota was the destination.

A plant there pumped water from the lake for use as a coolant. The water released back into the lake was warmer than the lake water. This increase in water temperature, for some reason, caused the white bass to congregate at the outlet.

The fishing was absolutely phenomenal. Virtually every cast produced a fish. In three days we caught more than seven hundred. In three nights we processed them all.

I was getting really tired of cleaning fish. But Dad had a rule: if you caught the fish you had to help clean them, all of them.

On the last day when Dad hollered for me to get up to go fishing, I stayed in bed. He was upset. I reminded him of his rule about cleaning fish; it logically followed that if I didn't catch any, I shouldn't have to clean any.

I went swimming instead and had a great time.

Not another word was said until we returned to the farm. The next day I was fueling up the Massey Harris tractor from the 300-gallon gasoline tank perched about six feet off the ground on a four-legged wooden stand leaning against a half-dead cottonwood tree on the west side of the scrap iron pile by the tool shop. Here came Dad, and he was still upset. For the next hour he scolded and shamed me over and over again for letting him down.

As I look back on this incident I ask, how could a father do this to his son? I was just a boy trying to deal with a complicated life. Occasionally I am asked whether or not I like fishing. Without exception my mind goes back to that day and I get a little sick to my stomach.

I have never been able to cover the pain of that incident with little more than a translucent scab.

I make little mention about my siblings as I write. For clarification it seems important to at least identify them. My sister, Linda, is one year older than me; my sister, Dianne, is two years younger; my brother, Gerry, is four years younger; my brother, Vern, is seven years younger; and my sister, Mary, is twelve years younger.

They too were affected by the way we were raised. Over the years as I have hurdled the obstacles in digging myself out of this hole, I have watched them struggle as well—not all in the same way, of course, and not all in same degree, but struggle just the same. I have no doubt they are all doing the best they can with the tools they have. I am even further convinced they have yet to comprehend the extent of the emotional damage done to them. As I stated earlier, it is easier to sweep it all under the rug only to perpetuate it into the next generation.

I am only laying the foundation to help you understand how my early life experience affected my ability to carry on successful relationships, with both Jean and our children. In writing this book I have grown to be less angry with my father. I try to look back on all of it with some degree of detachment. I obviously cannot change any of it. This is about what simply was.

I have always wondered to what extent Dad would have gone if he could not have gotten me under control with temper outbursts and verbal abuse. I never crossed that line until I met Jean. Numerous times he came at me as if he were going to beat me. But I stood my ground; although he raised his hand, he never struck. For some reason he drew the line.

By that time in my life I had the propensity to be just as angry and abusive as my father. Even though I knew it was wrong, I had no idea of the far-reaching, insidious nature of this beast and the war I would wage over the next forty years to overcome it. But overcome it, I did. Other than Jean, I know of no other person with the tenacity to dig through layer after layer to get to the bottom of this. I also do not know of another person who would continue to confront, confront, and confront to help me be the man I am today.

She is the one miracle in my life that dwarfs all others. She is the absolute love of my life, the most precious God-given gift I have ever received. Everything was not fine before she came along. But after she did, everything changed.

Here is the lesson: Your children are watching you. They will most likely become adults possessing the same attributes as you. If what they are learning is what I learned as a child, get some help. You can't fix this by yourself. And if you wait too long, the damage will already be done and you will have passed it all on to yet another generation. Stopping the buck begins with you.

22

LIVING WITH A BABE

Jean met my family for the first time when I invited her home for Easter Vigil Mass in the spring of 1970. My father took one look at her and, without saying a word, went to his bedroom and stayed there the rest of the evening. Of course in the usual dysfunctional manner in which we did things, Mom was the liaison between Dad and me.

Through her we learned that Jean's dress was too short and he was not about to have anything to do with a "woman like that." He was the prosecutor, judge, and jury, all wrapped into one. This left me in a tight spot. I thought Jean was the most wonderful person I had ever met, but my father would not even speak with her.

Here is the lesson: Had Jean been wise, she should have left the situation immediately, even if she had to walk, and never looked back. Knowing that I was a product of that environment, she should have realized I had a snowball's chance in hell of ever being anything other than a dismal failure when it came to being husband material. If this ever happens to you, do not walk, run. Guys like me, when I was nineteen, are not worth the effort.

I doubt it was her wardrobe that he found so objectionable but rather the threat she was to his authority. It seemed he wanted no one other than himself to exert any influence on his oldest son.

Most sons want their father's approval so badly that they would give almost anything for it. I was no different. My father wanted me to toss the love of my life overboard so he could once again be in total control. I simply would not do that. However, that does not make for a black-and-white situation. Time and time again I tried to get close to him, and time and time again it ended with abusive language and the demand for control. I lived between wanting so much to love Jean and knowing I had a father who seemed willing to sabotage that relationship in any way he could.

On the other hand, Jean was as tenacious as Dad. She was interested in a man, not a daddy's boy. She simply would not tolerate an allegiance to a father who acted out the way he did. Considering the amount of control he exerted, I find it difficult to understand why she continued the relationship. At times it was stormy, to say the least. But we hung in there and battled it out. It was never my intention to behave like my father. On the other hand overcoming twenty years of craziness was no small feat.

I was my father's son. The Weiland temper was notorious. Numerous times while I was a youth I heard mention of this. My grandfather's immediate family, along with their offspring, had a reputation for colossal temper outbursts. It was common knowledge that my great aunt threw boiling water at one of her children. Beating farm animals into a stupor was not uncommon on any of the Weiland farms.

Losing my temper was my normal reaction to anything I considered a personal assault, and there were many. Upon leaving our wedding dance we discovered our car windows covered with a layer of petroleum jelly. Removing it was almost impossible. It just smeared. I could not see to drive. Somehow, though, I managed to clear a twelve-inch-diameter hole in front of the driver's seat to see out.

I was livid. This was the first time I lost my temper during our married life. Jean took the whole incident in stride. Somehow I was able to cool down. The next day we went to a coin-operated car wash and removed the whole mess. No harm done. What I had felt as a personal assault was nothing more than an annoying prank.

During the first ten years of our marriage, losing my temper and taking it out on Jean was not unusual. As much as I knew this was wrong, I had virtually no skills to act any other way. I would get upset, lose my temper, blow off the pent-up energy, and apologize profusely for my outburst.

This cycle went on for years. This is the cycle of abuse and control I addressed in an earlier chapter. Sometimes I wouldn't lose my temper for a month or more. But as the stress of the farm crisis hit our family in the early eighties, it became a daily affair. I was angry all the time. I was angry at our financial situation. I was angry with Jean. I was angry with my dad. I was angry with the Catholic Church.

One night at the bottom of my life I sat on the couch stroking Jean's hair trying to make some amends with her after a particularly violent verbal outburst. As I sat next to her, I told her that we would be all right if we only had faith in God. A little later I left her side to use the restroom.

When I returned, I discovered she was gone. Because I could not leave the children, I could do nothing but wait. I was seething.

The next day she called with the ultimatum. I could either seek help for the anger or she would file for divorce. I did not realize it then but that was the first moment of the rest of my life.

In order to appease her, I called Catholic Family Services. I was able to get an appointment that very afternoon. Later Jean called again to see what my response would be. She agreed to meet me on a street corner in Madison. When I picked her up, she was wearing a snowmobile suit, stocking hat, and warm mittens. I remember thinking she was dressed to run. I had little doubt that she would.

Here is the lesson: It had taken Jean ten years to figure out what she should have known that night when she first visited the Weiland farm. I am stating this lesson twice because it is so important. Committing yourself with an abusive, controlling individual will make your life a living hell. If you have children together, it will even be worse. You most likely would live in poverty if you leave. If you stay, you will be teaching your children that the craziness is normal and acceptable. Remember the chance of these people changing is about as remote as winning the Powerball.

Together we attended the counseling session. I was an unwilling participant to say the least. To make matters worse, the counselor was a Catholic nun named Sister Claire. I only went because I knew it was the only way to keep Jean. After a psychological evaluation and a basic informal agreement, Jean agreed to come home. I at least had a reprieve.

Jean was not asked to return to counseling. I, on the other hand, continued the sessions. Sister Claire seemed to know everything about me. After about six weeks I had a vision of what needed to happen and willingly returned week after week. Later I attended an anger group with three other men—all with the same basic problems.

The difference between them and me was their refusal to accept responsibility for their behavior. It was here I learned the danger of a little phrase I coined to myself: "But if only she …" These guys seemed to know what it was they needed to do to save their families, but they continually stumbled on "but if only she"—but if only she would do whatever it was about their wife that they wanted to control. They never grew beyond that point. They all ended up in the divorce court.

For me, however, they gave me a chance to observe firsthand the devastation I was causing the people I loved most. I am in no way stating here that everything after that was smooth sailing. It was not. It was only the trailhead of a long and tenuous trek on which I stumbled over and over again, only to get up and start all over. Jean hung in there with me, although at times I still look back and wonder why.

Our son Carl was born on December 18, 1983. Outside, the snow was gently falling in huge flakes with a temperature approaching thirty below. After his birth,

Jean's uterus did not contract in the usual manner. The ensuing hemorrhage required an emergency transfusion with seven pints of blood.

After a couple days her situation normalized and we returned home to four older daughters, ages two to nine.

Jean was doing as well as could be expected. However, on Christmas Eve she once again began to hemorrhage profusely. I called the emergency unit. By the time she arrived at the hospital, her blood pressure had dropped to an extremely, dangerously low level. It was a dire situation.

The surgeons performed an emergency hysterectomy to stop the bleeding. In the process she required another eight pints of blood.

During the ordeal my dad and mom paced the hospital corridors with me praying for Jean to survive. I do not remember how long we did that. I remember preparing myself to be a widower with five very young children. I truly did not think at that moment she would survive. Considering all the setbacks we had had during the previous several years, the weight of this one seemed too great to bear.

As it was, she survived the surgery. However, her health did not return. The pain and fatigue she was experiencing was overwhelming. Looking back I still am amazed at how well she cared for the children. I simply do not know how she did it. I have a difficult time believing love like that to be common. We were broke: physically, financially, and certainly, at times, spiritually. There is no way to describe how challenging that situation was.

I had somehow always been able to dig up enough money to pay for our family medical insurance. This allowed us over the next several months to get the input of several area physicians. They all had varying opinions concerning the solution to Jean's illness. The last one we visited diagnosed her with an extreme case of arthritis.

> *Here is the lesson: Be careful with medical doctors, or any other professional for that matter. Some of them memorized their way through school, and some of them graduated at the bottom of their class. It seems to me it should be considered that, presently, the most incompetent medical doctor in the country may very well be misdiagnosing a life-threatening disease. Make sure you are not that patient.*

We didn't buy it. By May we had had enough. I made an appointment for Jean at the Mayo Clinic. The trip was difficult for her, but we needed some answers. After a battery of tests, Jean was diagnosed with pituitary insufficiency. This condition, if caused by postpartum hemorrhaging, is known as Sheehan's syndrome.

She was prescribed medications to replace the pituitary hormones her body no longer produced in a normal fashion. This somewhat improved her condition, but on average her life did not improve much. She spent so much energy taking care of our young children while I was out starting up the door company that she'd be completely exhausted by the end of the day. She was consistently weak. The pain in her muscles many times became almost unbearable.

A normal pituitary gland secretes cortisone, a brain chemical commonly known as adrenaline. The gland gives off this substance as the muscles in the body send messages that more or less is required. This function was lacking from Jean's body.

Every day she took a dose of prednisone, which is synthetic adrenaline. This was helpful, but giving her the correct dose was a guessing game at best. If she exerted too much physical effort during the day, her muscles ached profusely; if she exerted too little effort, she could not sleep. The dose was impossible to regulate correctly.

One other side effect of the disease was that her immune system was compromised. Because we had small children in school, she was often exposed to the various illnesses they brought home. So not only was she tired and fatigued from the difficulty in regulating the prednisone, she acquired every virus that passed by.

She was sick from these diseases most of the time. If I would get a cold or stomach flu and be over it in two days, Jean might have it for ten days or more. This was her life.

The damage her pituitary gland sustained following Carl's birth was extensive enough to make every day of her life a struggle. In addition to the chronic fatigue and sickness, Jean's blonde hair turned very dark brown. Her skin color changed from a normal pink to an ashen pale. My young wife looked years beyond her age.

She was so, so tired. I wonder why she fought so hard to live. I can only think that her love for us was so abiding that she could do nothing else.

In the spring of 1988 we learned of a lady and her husband who were traveling around the area. Their names were Pat and Ron Kremlacek. They were holding healing services in Catholic communities. When we discovered they were going to be at St. Mary's in Norfolk, Nebraska, we decided to go.

I was probably less optimistic than Jean, but anything that could help her physical condition was something worth trying.

That night turned out to be one of the most phenomenal spiritual experiences Jean and I have ever had. When we arrived at the church, we felt a calmness in the air. The music was soft. The people there, many who were physically incapacitated and sick, seemed to be anticipating something wonderful about to happen. We were forewarned that there would be things taking place that we may never have before experienced.

There was a talk explaining the different gifts of the Holy Spirit, especially the gifts of tongues and healing. During the service many people went to the front of the church to have the Kremlaceks pray for and lay hands upon them. I saw these people, while being touched during an incomprehensible prayer, simply fall over backward into the arms of a waiting attendant.

I certainly had my doubts. But when it became Jean's time for prayer, she simply collapsed. I thought it must be real. Jean never falls for anything phony.

And then it was my turn. Being touched that night was like being hit with a thunder bolt. There was a power unlike anything I had ever experienced—a gentle, wonderful, loving power. As I lay there, I was aware of all that was happening yet not willing or able to move.

After I got to my feet, Jean continued to lie quietly for a long time. No doubt she was resting in the arms of her Savior.

And I remembered the promise, "Leon I'm going to bless you with blessings you have never even dreamed of." I certainly had never dreamed of this.

Jean's physical healing did not happen immediately, but that service was the first event in a long period of recovery for Jean.

Jean and Pat Kremlacek became weekly prayer partners. Things were happening to her physically, little by little.

In August of that same year we went on a family vacation to Michigan. We had a wonderful time.

One night when we couldn't find a place to stay, our whole family of seven slept in our van. We were all so tired. Jean and the two youngest, Carl and Rebekah, slept on the cushions that were stretched horizontally across the back. Amber and Vanessa slept on the floor with their feet under the cushions where Jean and the youngest children were. Stephanie and I slept in the captain's chairs in the front.

By 2:00 a.m. we were still not sleeping. We were so tired that the kids started to get goofy. Amber started to giggle at our predicament, and we all followed suit. It was a funny place to be.

We were all together. As a family we were one and we loved each other. We laughed and sang songs until finally, one by one, we drifted to sleep. What a great night. That experience was one of the best family times we ever had—at least it was for me.

Life is what you make of it. Our family made lemonade from lemons that night in a 1982 Chevrolet conversion van in a remote campground in Traverse City, Michigan.

But that wasn't the most profound experience of that vacation. A couple days later we were on Mackinac Island, which is located in a strait that connects Lake Huron and Lake Michigan. It is a beautiful area with its shops and tourist attractions.

As we were strolling around, Jean noticed a bicycle rental place. She insisted that we bicycle around the perimeter of the island, which I recall to be about six miles. I was irritated. Why would someone in her physical condition think it wise to ride a bike that far? But she was absolutely insistent. And so we rented the bicycles.

Everyone had their own bike except the youngest, Carl, who was only four at the time and who rode in a seat on the back of my bicycle. The scenery was spectacular. The sun was out and the water in the lake was as blue as the sky. The wind whisked our faces as we biked all the way around the island, Jean included.

This at first does not seem to be any spectacular event. But considering that my Jean rode a bicycle six miles without any physical hindrance was an absolute miracle. A year earlier this bike ride would have nearly killed her. But it didn't. In fact the next day she was doing fine and experiencing no adverse effects, no muscle aches. This was almost unbelievable.

The next month, in September, Jean began to feel a different kind of illness. She just felt bad all over. I was scared. Jean and I visited her endocrinologist. He did several blood tests and came to the conclusion that he did not believe Jean needed to continue taking the prednisone.

I was skeptical. A couple years earlier, the doctors at the Mayo Clinic tried this same approach. Within two days of stopping the medication, she was in so much pain she could barely get out of bed.

I remember asking the doctor if he was sure of what he was doing and told him the story about when stopping the medication had been tried earlier. He asked us to trust his opinion, and we reluctantly did.

This happened on a Tuesday. He asked Jean to take a half dose on the following Friday and Saturday, no dose on the following Sunday and Monday, and come in for further testing on Tuesday. After the two half-dose days, she felt fine. After the no-dose days she felt even better. The tests on Tuesday proved she no longer needed to take the prednisone. We were ecstatic. This was tremendous.

CT scans later showed her pituitary gland to be of normal size. Three years earlier the same test showed it to be atrophied and abnormally small.

Her hypothyroidism was still present. However, this is much easier to regulate than the low adrenal function.

A miraculous healing was happening. Her hair turned back to her normal color and her skin was no longer as pale as it had been for so long. And again I remembered the promise.

We took this as a sign that Jean was on the road to recovery. That bike ride was the first indication that her body was more receptive to physical activity. During the next two years Jean did exhausting physical therapy to rebuild her atrophied muscles caused by the side effects of prednisone and years of limited physical activity.

Even though she had more energy, she continued to be attacked by one viral infection after another. This was her life for the next fifteen years.

In 2001, after a visit to her endocrinologist, Jean was somewhat frustrated because she believed she was not receiving a correct amount of thyroid medication.

I began doing some research on her condition via the Internet. I discovered a physician in Omaha who specialized in hormone replacement therapy. His thinking was somewhat outside the box, but after getting the same song and dance from doctor after doctor for almost twenty years, we thought a change in philosophy might be advisable.

In addition to correcting her thyroid difficulties, he diagnosed Jean with what he thought was the lowest level of human growth hormone he'd ever seen in a live person.

He prescribed an injectable growth hormone. It took about six months from when she started taking injections before she felt significantly better, but slowly her HGH level began to build to normal levels. She no longer contracted so many of the viral infections. She was doing so much better. She finally had her life back!

Jean's recovery took a long time, twenty years or more. But through it all, I never lost sight of the fact that she was still the same beautiful woman I had come to know all those years earlier outside the junior college gym. I've been blessed to live with my beautiful Jean for my entire adult life, and it's been an experience I wouldn't trade for the world. As the Lady Antebellum song states, "She'll always be eighteen and beautiful and dancing away with my heart."

I believe most men, if they were honest, would admit their desire to live with a beautiful woman. I also believe it is helpful, if not essential, for a woman to be loved and cared for to be as beautiful as she can be. I think it is possible for a woman to lose her attractiveness due to her husband's neglect. No doubt God loves our wives unconditionally in ways far beyond our understanding. It would seem an appropriate prayer that we would ask Him to help us strive to love them as he does and to see them as the beautiful people they truly are.

Taking care of that special person is absolutely the most fundamental job of any man who is married. Yet I have watched otherwise respectable men bully and deprive their wives as if she was little more than a slave, insisting she ask or beg for any crumb he might throw her way. Any man who has an attitude like this might consider that his wife has the option of divorce, in which "his" so called assets will most likely be split down the middle.

> *Here is the lesson: Look up the definition of the word* **bully.** *Webster defines one as "a blustering browbeating person; especially: one habitually cruel to others who are weaker." When relating to the one whom you once thought of as a dream come true, consider whether the way you are doing it is appropriate for that special person.*

Consider as well that there are those of us who are sensitive enough to pick you out of a crowd. You expose yourself by your words, your voice intonations, your actions and inactions, and your attitude.

If you are one of those little people who self-inflate because of your ability to control others, please consider that there are those of us who have expended our lives cleaning up the s--t left in the wake of your selfish, insensitive habits.

It is somewhat embarrassing for me to expound on the value of treating your woman in a caring, respectful way. I have neglected writing this part of the book for just that reason. However, if I wait until I am perfect to write it, it will never be said, at least not by me. My posterity would never know how hard I fought to overcome this difficulty.

As a husband I have often failed miserably. I doubt there is any man reading this book who has been a worse husband than I had been. When I am good, I'm really good. On the other hand, when I have been bad, the extreme opposite has also been true.

For most of my married life I have struggled to stomp out the effects of my childhood. I have read numerous books on the subject of being a better husband simply to use that knowledge to be controlling of Jean. It is possible to have a mountain of intellectual knowledge while struggling with the relational skills required for putting it all together.

However, every so often I was able to climb up another step to overcome yet another control issue, little by little peeling off the layers. The untrusting, backward way of relating that I learned as a child has proven to be almost impossible to overcome. Sometimes I wonder why Jean ever put up with me all these years other than she could not help but notice how hard I tried to get it right. I never have for very long without falling on my face.

It has been my observation that whether it's a husband or a boyfriend, girls want their significant others to treat them like the beautiful people they are. It has been my experience that most women appreciate having doors opened for them, receiving compliments about their appearance, full gas tanks in their cars, tidy rooms in their homes, and the occasional love note to remind them they're cared for. It's important for men to make sure they let their women know they think she is really something, a real "babe" if you will. If she doesn't feel like one, it seems to me, it would be difficult for her to be one.

This works both ways in relationships. However, I'm putting the emphasis on the behavior of the male side because women, typically being natural nurturers, respond favorably to a man who cares for them. From my observations it seems the vast majority of failed marriages are caused by husbands who neglect the emotional needs of their families.

On the other hand, women, if you want your husband to step up to the plate, don't ever let him forget he's your man. Perhaps nothing is more important in a marriage than both partners feeling appreciated by their spouse. To really make a marriage work, or any relationship for that matter, both partners must act to let each other know that they're appreciated. Over the course of a marriage, feelings may come and go, but the commitment to each other has to remain a constant.

Here is the lesson: Living with a babe depends much on your attitude. If it is one of self-centeredness, you most likely will never have the experience. You and your beautiful wife will both be the losers. So buck up and get to work.

Here is the lesson: "Bask in the love of that beautiful someone who has chosen you and willingly gives their life for your love."

I think this is rather profound. We are continuously bombarded with sex as a performance or the means to something. How often do we just wallow in the love of another and enjoy the pleasure and intimacy to which that leads? I have never read anything like this on the cover of Cosmo—*most likely because it does not exist in the realm where they preach. As much as that ilk would refuse to believe this, this is what you find in church. This, it would seem, is significant with what God wants to have with us.*

After dinner one evening our Russian daughter, Leysan, was perched on a stool across from me at the eating bar at the lake house. She was snickering as she scrolled through some e-mails on her laptop. Curious, I nonchalantly asked her, "What do you think?"

She replied, "I think you and Jean have a purposeful life."

I was somewhat startled by her reply. However it did give me cause to consider what prompted her to answer.

As an adolescent boy one of my chores was milking the cow. To do this I had to coax her into the stanchion with a mixture of corn and oats, which she couldn't eat without putting her head between the bars. When she did, I would lock it closed, then she munched on the grain as I milked her by hand. We did not have a machine for this chore. It simply was not feasible for just one cow. I sat on a stool which, when I was first old enough to do this job, was no more than a fifteen inch two-by-four with a twelve-inch board nailed to one end forming a T.

This makeshift stool worked somewhat satisfactorily. However it was difficult to balance because it had only one leg. As time went on, I fabricated a stool with four legs that didn't work well either. Because the barn floor was uneven, the stool rocked back and forth on two of the legs and one of the others. This gave me an idea. The next one I made had three legs, all of which, when I sat on it, were planted firmly on the floor. How, you might ask, does this have anything to do with a purposeful life? My answer is quite simply, plenty!

Over the years I have observed that life experience can be divided into three areas. All of them intertwined and working together; however, no different from the three legs of the stool, if any one of those areas is neglected, that life will be less than balanced. In the barn if the balance on my milking stool, was too far off kilter I might land in the gutter with my face covered with cow crap. In real life if you fall off the stool, the outcome can be even worse.

From my observation, along with my own life experience, I believe the three stool legs of a purposeful life are spiritual, social, and physical. To me the most important of these three is the spiritual part. It would follow that, unlike the others, this this part would have eternal consequences.

My faith experience causes me to believe we, as humans, are created in the image and likeness of God, and since we possess the senses of hearing, sight, taste, and feeling, I think we will eternally have those same senses. Let me say this again. It makes perfect sense, to me, that we will have the ability to feel happy, sad, heat, cold, loneliness, along with fear, torment, and terror. If life with God is the eternal experience of all that is lovable—where fear, torment, and terror have no place to reside—how does it not make sense that there is a hell where they can?

Maybe you've heard the story of a bird that flew to a tall mountain where it pecked at its rocky ledges for five minutes and flew away, only to return once every year, year after year, to peck away for another five minutes. Eternity, it seems, could be defined as the equivalent of the time it would take for that little bird to peck that mountain to the level of the plains below.

It follows, to me, that a life begins the moment of our conception and ends when the bird finishes the work on the mountain. I find this to be absolutely awesome. So in consideration of a purposeful life, the choices we make in the beginning will affect the outcome later. In this case the opposite of beginning is not the end. The opposite of beginning is eternity. Whether it is eternally wonderful or eternally horrifying is up to you. Individual belief, yours or mine, in this concept is inconsequential.

Again, to ponder this correctly, it would seem one would want to further put this idea into a context that would have a common understanding. I doubt anyone reading this has not played or at least heard of the lottery. How many have plopped down a few bucks for a one-in-a-billion chance of winning? This leads me to the question: what are the chances that there is an eternal hell? Is the reality of that better than winning the lottery? In this instance I refer to hell, instead of heaven, because any semblance of a purposeful life definitely would not include any part of hell.

The old adage, "Life can be Hell," would certainly confirm this. There are many who are betting their eternity that there is no eternity; to me, this would be a bet not to lose. I don't want to be remiss in failing to propose the possibility.

Again, referring back to my faith experience, which causes me to believe there is a God in heaven who is the epitome of all that is lovable, good, clean, pure, and powerful, and we are made in his image and likeness, how could our purpose not be in step with all that he is? How does it not make perfect sense that the first leg of the stool be all that is spiritual? To have a truly purposeful life, one would have to have desire for what we cannot see with our eyes.

How well we relate to God in a way that is pleasing to him would seem most important in our quest for social balance. Note I did not say "relate to God in a way that makes me feel good." That, it seems, would be considered a quest for pleasure, not a quest for holiness. On the other hand, walking on that path certainly has a way of causing that to happen.

From what I have learned, Jesus was a man of suffering. As he walked the earth he had no place to lay his head. That was his choice. Earthly comfort was not his mission. His mission was to gather all of us, his children, to himself like a hen gathers her chicks under her wing, if you will. If we are in fact like those chicks, that area under her wing is not spacious. Somehow, being together in that little space would require us to find a way to hold onto each other, to bear each other up. That is the challenge of the social leg of the stool.

I heard a story about a woman who, after hearing a speech given by Mother Teresa of Calcutta, was so inspired that she wanted to do great things to serve others. Upon relating her newfound desire to Mother Teresa, she was asked whether she had a family.

The woman responded, "Yes, of course."

Mother Teresa said, "Then go home and be their mother."

Go home and be their mother; go home and be their father, go to your neighbor and be their friend. Rejoice at another's success. Be glad in the goodness of others. Be a good example to the children in your community. Do not harbor resentments and jealousies. Be patient with another's failures. Give care to those who are sick, and understanding to those who are emotionally depressed. Bear each other's faults in humility.

This thinking, it seems, is so absolutely counter to the urging of our secular society that it is rarely considered a remedy for contention. Consider how everything around us might change if we took this "it's-all-my-fault attitude" and whittled away at our attachment to secular thinking. The social leg of a purposeful life would surely, I would think, include an eye toward heaven and all that entails, along with attention to the care of others.

The spiritual and social legs of the stool will do much to garner a purposeful life. However, they encompass more of that which is a disposition of person. They are that which causes us to desire intimate connection with God and others. On the other hand, the third leg is the physical response that causes one to gather that which holds it all together. This is work.

Merriam-Webster's Dictionary calls it "sustained physical or mental effort to overcome obstacles and achieve an objective or result." In the physical world nothing happens without this. Just like the nails and screws that were required in order to hold my little three-legged stool together, work is required in order to bring value to all the legs. Without it the others will be much less than effective. It is rather difficult to convince anyone of the value of the first two legs if they are physically deprived. And they will be physically deprived without that which is gained with work. This leg is about money and what it will buy.

If a child says, "Mommy, Mommy, my tummy hurts. May I have something to eat?"

And the mother replies, "I have two church meetings today. Tomorrow I am going on retreat. Maybe I will have time to grocery shop the day after that. In the meantime, have some potato chips and soda. I'll be finished with this Altar Society schedule in a little bit. Maybe then we can say your night prayers together."

Of course this is an exaggeration. But it demonstrates that too much of any leg will cause the stool to tip over. You see the child was hungry. It would be difficult for him to gather much appreciation for night prayers. It would be more possible for that child to gain a disdain for anything having to do with this activity. In addition, he would be learning a distorted view of how a mother should care for her children. Father Ryberg described persons such as this as "being so heavenly minded that they are of little earthly good."

I have had the inclination lately to ask people I meet: "What is your dream?" Almost invariably they respond that their dream is to be exceedingly rich. And when I ask them how they intend to achieve that, they mostly respond in one of three ways, either they do not have a clue, by not doing what they are doing, or third, winning the lottery. All three answers, it seems, demonstrate a certain amount of futility. Sadly, our secular culture has glamorized extreme financial wealth to the point where it is the pinnacle of desire, yet completely out of reach. It seems especially so for those to whom it most likely is remote, at best.

I have encountered several situations in my life where the desire for things that only excessive wealth can buy was so enticing that folks were duped into acting in ways that caused them to lose all or some of what they had. These people simply failed to understand that financial rewards invariably match the value of the work involved. When little actual work is required, there is little chance of winning the prize.

Not long after Jean and I were married, I worked as an account rep for a financial services company. Our business was making personal loans. During that time, there was a pyramid scheme being circulated in which people were being sold the idea that if they would buy into this business for a mere thousand dollars, they would be on their way to wealth and happiness. In order to further this cause, the people promoting this scheme organized a rally at a local auditorium where anyone who had bought into this idea could bring their friends and family in order to persuade them to do the same.

For this purpose, several people had applied to us for loans. I thought it wise to know what was going on. Before the age of the Internet, there were limited means available to research things like this. The whole scheme seemed rather fishy, so Jean and I decided to attend.

As we entered the rally we encountered festive music. People chanting, "Money! Money! Money!" Their arms were in the air and hands clapping. It was an absolute frenzy. The leaders were impeccably dressed in eveningwear with rhinestone American flags pinned to their lapels. It was a sight to see and an experience to be had. As we stood there with our arms crossed, we were an anomaly and not well received. Shortly after, we left.

Through our business connections I knew many of these hard-working middle-class folks, commonly living from paycheck to paycheck. Many had no idea what it was like to own a brand new car, and certainly had little reason to own an evening gown or a fancy suit. However, they had supposedly seen the glitz that money could buy and they wanted it. What they didn't realize was that what they were seeing was mostly a façade. This was especially so among the crowd putting on the show that evening.

The other situations went like this. During the first several years after I started the door company, I was acquainted with two individuals who had bought into this idea. The first invariably carried a roll of one-dollar bills in his pocket wrapped with a hundred dollar bill, which gave the impression that the whole roll was made of hundreds. He lived in an old rundown house, but he was always impeccably dressed as he made the rounds in a very expensive automobile. He flattered any and everyone, but fooled only a few. My friend, Jim Housel, jokingly called his business C & D Sales. C & D were acronyms for confuse and deceive. He used whoever he could to perpetuate his lie. The sad part in all of this was that he was remarkably talented. He passed up numerous opportunities because it would have forced him to give up this phony outward show. Because of this he lost his inherited farm, his lovely wife, and his business. A few years later he died lonely and broke.

The second fellow inherited a thriving business. He too was amazingly talented. He could dissect and understand the mechanical workings of about anything. In addition, his talent for metal fabrication was remarkable. But he too bought into this idea of spending way beyond his means. He bled the business of cash by indulging foreign luxury automobiles, high living, and a large hilltop home on the outskirts of town.

At the same time he was draining cash from his business, the need for the products he produced decreased because of changes in the agricultural sector demographics. As those changes occurred, he complained about the changing climate but did little to accommodate what was happening until it was too late. He borrowed large sums of money to accommodate the outgo of cash from his business as he laid off his salespeople. In the end a natural disaster halted the downhill slide. The bank repossessed his cars and foreclosed on his business and his beautiful home.

In all three of these situations, the people failed to understand that in any activity when the intended rewards do not match the work required, they are most likely pipe dreams at best. Instead of becoming that which holds the rest together, they become that which causes the whole stool to topple over, likely taking some or all of the spiritual and social legs along with it.

Both of these individuals mistakenly thought that excessive monetary wealth was the biggest and most important leg of the stool. Or perhaps the only one required. So much so that even a false sense of it was better than none. I have never seen this idea be successful. This thinking tends to destroy that which should be considered as reasonable, an amount large enough to adequately provide for the financial security necessary to allow spiritual and social connection.

The word *enough* is defined as "that which is required to satisfy a need." It seems to me this word is considered far too sparingly. When is it enough? Could it be when the spiritual leg, the social leg, and the physical leg are somewhat matched in size and length? Enough to allow these three areas of our lives to be somewhat balanced and in order.

For me, however, I have never attained a perfect balance. At best, it has been somewhat balanced. In this endeavor, I am continually pressing on. In reality, my life has been more balanced like a see-saw, teetering from one side to the other and once in a while metaphorically crashing like the time Wally Schlenz decided to get off when I was at the high end. Even at that, on average I think it has been pretty good.

No doubt Jean and I have a purposeful life. The promise made to me years ago has been kept. I am equally sure the whole of it has yet to be revealed. Our journey has been fraught with failure, disappointment, tough times that came close to tearing us apart, depression, sickness, and cancer. Yet every morning we strive to begin again. You see, at our house we believe in love. That is what ultimately wraps us all together. That is what we seek, in our own feeble, misguided and sometimes really "dumb" way. As for me? At times I get self-assured that we have all the legs working well together only to find it was the love of God and others, especially Jean, faithfully accommodating one short leg after the other. God bless!!

Here is the lesson: Seek love. Believe in it. That is your purpose. In that you will be all you can be. In the end that is all there is.

ABOUT THE AUTHOR

As a young farmer, Leon Weiland, along with his wife and best friend, Jean, was caught between the forces of escalating debt and rabid increase in interest rates. The situation left them six figures in the red. At the crescendo of their financial difficulties, Jean gave birth to their fifth child. The delivery was complicated at best. The aftermath left her, the mother of five between the ages of newborn and nine, lethargic, weak and chronically in pain. As the lone breadwinner of this brood, along with limited skills and little formal higher education Weiland turned down a job with the US Postal Service in order to pursue an idea given to him by a friend and former employer—that of building fiberglass doors for the food industry.

Four years later Jean was partially healed of her malady enough to effectively function as a mother. Together Leon and Jean have built a powerhouse for good as Weiland Doors are listed on the spec sheets of world-class companies throughout the United States. The business which has now has been turned over to the next generation continues to grow in ways which brings wholesomeness to the Weiland Family. In *Smell the Dirt*, Mr. Weiland chronicles his life journey from an impoverished childhood to the man he has become; along with the steps in between and the lessons he has learned.

PHOTO ALBUM

Leon at about 1 year old

Leon at about 4 years old with shiny
new dump truck, Christmas at Grandma
Goodwater's house

Sister Linda and Leon with Grandpa
Weilands old Dodge pickup truck

Leon with a bee sting
above left eye 5 years old

Sisters Linda and Dianne,
Leon about 1954

Leon, brother Gerry, sisters Dianne and Linda,
and Grandma Goodwater

Cousin Don Goodwater, sister Linda and
Leon practicing mud pie culinary arts

Weiland sisblings with several
Goodwater cousins

Brother Vernon bottle feeding a lamb
in front of farm house

Grandma Goodwater, sister
Linda and Leon

Left to right back row, Sisters Linda and Dianne
along with Leon, Gerry in front feasting on
watermelon in late summer

Grandma Goodwater striking a funny pose
while cutting meat in the kitchen

(Left to right) Siblings Gerry, Dianne, Leon, Linda and Vernon along with pet lambs about 1961

(Left to right) Siblings Gerry, Leon, Dianne and Linda about 1962

Family photo 1965

Family photo 1967

Leon in sisth grade, 1963

Leon's highschool senior portrait

Leon's highschool graduation, 1969

Leon's mother, Viola Weiland,
mid to late 1930's

Parents Viola and Gilbert Weiland costumed for the
annual Firemans Masquerade Dance, late 1960's

Leon's parents, Viola and Gilbert Weiland, 1998

Jean and Leon, Easter 2005

Made in the USA
Middletown, DE
23 October 2016